# The Swedish Wage Negotiation System

Abstract

Anders S. Olsson 1990. The Swedish Wage Negotiation System. 179 pages.

This book examines the structural formation and reformation of the Swedish wage negotiation system and the role collective actors play in these processes. Particular attention is paid to 'The Swedish Model' of centralized wage negotiation and administration. The theoretical-methodological aim is to specify several key organizing principles which give the system its identifying properties and stability. Factors which destabilize the system and set the stage for transition to other systems are also examined. Different analytical models are associated with four different epochs, each with its particular negotiation system, after 1945.

The wage rounds between 1980 and 1986 are analyzed and the linkages between the organizations in the labor market are discussed. Close attention is given to the development of wage development guarantees. The circumstances leading up to the decentralization of wage negotiations in 1983 are also discussed.

Wage drift is one of the destabilizing factors affecting the central wage negotiation system. Wage drift is seen as the result of local bargaining processes where: 1) Profits play a role. 2) Product markets rather more than labor markets are seen to influence wage drift developments. 3) Comparisons of relative wage gains through reference networks spread wage drift. 4) Piece-wages are a vehicle for wage drift by giving ample opportunities for bargaining over centrally established rates.

It is suggested that conflicts between different unions in Sweden are partly based on different conceptions of distributive justice. It is argued that there exist differences among the members of different unions. Strong support was found for the principle of distributive justice which emphasizes the notion of responsibility in work. It is argued that the dominant principle of distributive justice reflects the development of the economy and the work places.

*Anders S. Olsson, Department of Sociology, Box 513, S-751 20 Uppsala, Sweden.*

Reprint of a doctoral dissertation at Uppsala University

# The Swedish Wage Negotiation System

Anders S. Olsson

Uppsala 1990
Department of Sociology
Uppsala University

Dartmouth

Published by
Dartmouth Publishing Company Limited
Gower House
Croft Road
Aldershot
Hants  HU11 3HR

Dartmouth Publishing Company
Old Post Road
Brookfield
Vermont 05036
USA

ISBN 1 85521 203 X

Printed in Great Britain by
Billing & Sons Ltd, Worcester

# Contents

# List of Tables

# List of Figures

# Acknowledgements

This study of the Swedish Wage Negotiation System was made possible through a grant from *The Bank of Sweden Tercentenary Foundation*. The research group, which has consisted of professor Tom R. Burns, research assistants Madeleine Wänseth and Tuula Eriksson, has contributed with inspiration and critique.

Tom R. Burns together with Pablo Suaréz have been my advisors at the Department of Sociology. Several of the chapters have been discussed at the Political Sociology Seminar where Sten Anttila, Gladys Golborne, Jorge Calbucura, Jorge Dresdner, Kenneth Asp, Anne-Marie Kallikoski have taken their time to read and criticize my papers. I have also received valuable comments from Michael Thålin, Eva Meyerson, Richard Swedberg, Steve Turner, Steve Minett (who also corrected my English) , Göran Brulin, Agneta Hugemark, and Håkon Leiulfsrud.

Many others have contributed in various ways. I want to thank Nils Elvander, Christian Nilsson, Karl-Olof Faxén and Ingvar Ohlsson.

I also want to thank all my friends and colleagues at the Sociology department who have contributed to a supportive and critical atmosphere.

This work is dedicated to my wife, Anna-Karin and my daughter Annika.

Uppsala August 1990

*Anders S. Olsson*

# Preface

The various attempts to theorize about industrial relations each emphasize different aspects of the relationship between employers and employees. The one thing in common is the subject matter: industrial relations.[1] In chapter one I discuss the theoretical basis for the different approaches to the study of industrial relations. I also discuss the role of rules in industrial relations theories.

Chapter two deals with the changes in the wage negotiation system. An earlier version of this chapter has been published in collaboration with Tom R. Burns in Burns and Flam (1987). The post war system of wage negotiations is analyzed as a set of rule regimes. I examine the structural formation and reformation of the Swedish wage bargaining system, particularly 'The Swedish Model' of centralized wage negotiation and administration. The theoretical-methodological focus is on identifying key organizing principles which give each system its identifying properties and stability, at the same time that institutional failures of, and emerging struggles around, established principles destabilize the system and set the stage for transition to other systems. The period is divided up into four epochs depending on the key rules of the dominating rule regime. The actors in the central arena are seen as major factors influencing the formation of a rule regime. The development of the bargaining system is also seen as dependent on the formation of power resources in actual bargaining situations.

In chapter three I describe the Swedish system of wage negotiations. The developments during the eighties are investigated. I introduce the actors and discuss some of the most outstanding features of the system. Here the focus is placed on the linkages between the negotiations as they developed in the rules for collective agreements. Attention is given to the specific development of the negotiation context. This chapter builds on a research report published in 1984 together with Madeleine Wänseth.

Chapter four analyzes the phenomena of wage drift (the deviation from central collective agreements). The focus is on the role of local unions and managements as actors in the wage drift process. The rules of wage systems are seen as important instruments facilitating wage drift and easing its spread. The resources at the actors disposal is seen to enable them to initiate wage drift. In addition, the Economic theories of wage drift are presented and criticized. The theoretical importance of labor market competition for the occurrence of wage drift is challenged and an alternative explanation is offered.

In chapter five it is argued that the principles of distributive justice which can be found in the wage structure, conceptions, and policies of the unions and among the Swedish population, reflect significant differences between groups of employees, and that there are significant differences between white-collar workers and blue-collar workers. The prevailing principle, that of 'responsibility' is argued to reflect the hierarchization of work-places and the growth of internal labor markets.

# 1 Toward a Theory of Industrial Relations and Collective Bargaining

## The Systems Model

Industrial relations systems theory has largely focused on rules and rule making. Dunlop (1958) tried to explain the rules within the industrial relations system with concepts such as technology, market constraints, and the distribution of power. While market constraints were considered to be the decisive factor in determining the rules in the industrial-relations system, technology shapes the production and has an impact on the localization of work, working conditions and much more. The locus and distribution of power in the larger society does not directly determine the interaction of the actors in the industrial relations system. Dunlop saw it rather as a context which helps to structure the industrial-relations system itself.

The actors in such an industrial-relations system consist, according to Dunlop, of a hierarchy of managers, a hierarchy of workers, and specialized governmental agencies. His focus is on the rules in the industrial-relations system. These coexist in a 'web of rules' in which he distinguishes between three kinds of rules: procedures for establishing rules, substantive rules, and procedures for deciding their application to particular situations.[2]

The procedures for establishing rules may be maintained by any combination of managers, workers representatives, and government agencies. The substantive rules may govern compensation, duties of workers, and rights of workers. The growing complexity of the rules makes their application more difficult and the need arises for experts to perform this function.[3]

Dunlop adopted the premise that rule-bound action is (exhaustively) constitutive of concrete social action. This was embedded in the systems approach formalized by Parsons and Smelser. Commons had earlier challenged neo-classical economics and had elaborated a conception of rule-bound or non-rational action in markets, while avoiding Mayo's radical non-rationalism.[4] Dunlop used these ideas in order to adopt an approach where explanations were given in terms of *system needs or goals* rather than the purposes of the actors. He assumed that there must be an integrative function in the system, in this case a common ideology.

Dunlop sees the normal case as one where there exists a consensus which allows for the maintenance of the system. His formulation does allow for changes when the consensus breaks down. If one so to say periodizes Dunlop, he can be interpreted in a dynamic fashion. This does not prevent his approach from becoming no more than comparative statics. He fails to see the system as continuously evolving due to the different ideologies of the actors, their strategies to change the system, and their power-resources needed to accomplish such a change.

Flanders (1969) saw, like Dunlop, that rule-bound action is constitutive of concrete social action. Flanders was not, however, committed to systems analysis. The collective agreement is, according to Flanders, not an ordinary bargain but an agreement on what rules to apply in industrial relations.

In contrast to collective bargaining, bargaining, according to Flanders, is defined as 'the process by which the antithetical interest of supply and demand, of buyer and seller, are finally adjusted' so as to end 'in the act of exchange'.[5] Only the individual bargain between an employer and an employee accords with this definition. Collective bargaining is something different:

> A collective agreement, on the other hand, though it is frequently called a collective bargain and in some countries where it has legal force a collective contract, does not commit anyone to buy or sell labour. It does something quite different. It is meant to ensure that when labour is bought and sold (the specific kinds of labour referred to) its price and the other terms of the transaction will accord with the provisions of the agreement. These provisions are in fact a body of rules intended regulate among other things the terms of employment contracts. Thus collective bargaining is itself essentially a rule-making process, and this is a feature which has no proper counterpart in individual bargaining.[6]

The relationship between employers and employees, is according to Flanders, a power relationship. From this he draws the conclusion that collective barganing is primarily a political institution.[7]

Flanders keeps the rule-concept while avoiding the quagmire of functionalistic system theory. In the following section, I will try to expound an approach to studying industrial relations with rule-concepts which allows for power and conflict and does not force the analyst to assume underlying consensus for the system.

# Toward a Sociology of Negotiation Processes

### Rule Regimes, their formation and reformation: The Theory of Social Rule Systems

Dunlop endeavored to explain why different kinds of rules existed in different situations depending on external factors such as technology, market constraints and distribution of power. But rules can also be seen as tools available to actors, as well as results from conflicts and negotiations. It is possible to partially bridge social action and social structure without having to presuppose a normative consensus through contemporary theoretical developments such as structuration theory.[8] The latter, in particular provides an over-arching language which permits communication between the different schools of industrial relations theory.

The theory focuses on two fundamental rule processes, 1) the formation and reformation of social rule systems; 2) the implementation of social rules, which may involve the mobilization of power and authority to enforce rules.[9] Organizational, administrative, economic and political institutions are special types of rule systems which are called *rule regimes*. These are enforced through networks of control in which sanctions can be applied. In a rule system such as the Swedish wage negotiation system, the use of power resources is not totally unrestricted. In most cases the exercise of power takes place within a social system, and is guided by rules. The rules, laws, and forms of action which structure and regulate a negotiation system constitutes a rule regime.[10]

Actors may focus on certain rules and try to change them in order to increase their power or for other reasons. The power to change the rule regime is called meta-power.[11] Rules should not be considered determinant. Social rules are transgressable; it is possible to refrain from adhering to them, or to give them new interpretations.

Figure 1.1:    A Model of Multi-level Social System[12]

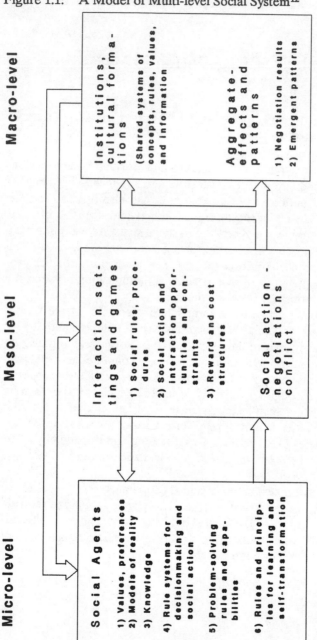

Social actors are the bearers of rule systems. Different groups or actors can combine their efforts in shaping and maintaining specific systems of rules. Actors may clash on the basis of their different interests with respect to the maintenance or change of the rule system. Social actors have different values, preferences, models of reality. They also have different rules for decision making, problem-solving, and learning. With these properties actors participate in negotiation contexts and games which are governed by social rules and procedures. Interaction settings have specific action and interaction opportunities and constraints, as well as reward and cost structures. Finally all participate in larger institutional settings and other cultural formations, which consist of shared systems of concepts, rules, values and information.[13]

> [the theory]... concerns the formation and implementation of social rule systems. *The rule systems governing transactions among agents in a defined sphere specify to a greater or lesser extent who participates* (and who is excluded), *who does what, when, where, and how, and in relation to whom.* In particular, they define possible rights and obligations, including rules of command and obedience, governing specified categories of actors or roles vis a vis one another. *The theory deals with the properties of social rule systems, their role in patterning social life, and the social and political processes whereby such systems are produced, maintained, and transformed as well as implemented* in social action and interaction.[14]

Human agents adhere to social rule systems for three purposes: 1) To organize, coordinate, and regulate their interactions, both for collective and individual purposes. 2) To organize their perceptions, interpretations and understandings of what is going on, providing a certain degree of inter-subjectivity and enabling knowledgeable actors to roughly simulate and predict certain patterns. 3) To refer to in giving ccounts and engaging in normative discourse about what is or should be going on, justifying and criticizing actions and outcomes.

The rule regimes of the production process also enter into the negotiation process as a restricting force and as a resource for tactical action for the actors. Business economics and national economic policy enters in as rule systems, as a basis to judge what actions are beneficial or detrimental for the individual firm or for the economy as a whole.

Important for the maintenance of a rule-regime is the ability to uphold specific organizing principles and rules. This ability may stem from material resources possessed by the actors or from moral values which the actors refer to as sources of legitimation. A rule without such backing is not likely to survive. The unique character of the 'private' rule regime of the wage negotiation system depends on the large power resources possessed by the actors, which to a certain extent balance the power of the state.

One most important aspect of rules and rule systems is what they do not proscribe. This field of indetermination I will call the *free-zone*. If no such zone existed, then rules would fully determine social life. The free-zones are necessary for the function of rule systems. The multitude of social life presents such variation that to control it fully with rules would demand a lot of rules making the control itself very complex, or it would take a large repressive apparatus to enforce behavior within those rules which exist. In systems theory there is *the law of requisite variety* which states (simplified) that *only variety can destroy variety*.[15] Thus, trying to control social phenomena through rule systems in most cases leaves som area of discretion, some alternatives of action that are not controlled through rules. It is however the rules which decide where the free-zone is going to be, or what it is going to look like. The rules does this through what they do not regulate.

I suggest that any rule system is dependent on its free-zone for its survival and legitimacy. A rule system without a free-zone would determine all aspects of actions. Such a system would be unbareable for those who have to live under it. System malfunctions would not be possible to evade. Since human rationality is limited, malfunctions will arise in most systems. The free-zone may act as a valve which allows to adjust actions so as to counteract such malfunctions, and thus making the rule system easier to cope with. One of the questions in changing or designing a rule system should thus be: What actions and what staes should be left unregulated? A too small free-zone may undermine the legitimacy of the rule system. A too large free-zone may also prove counterproductive in the sense that it undermines the regulating intent behinf the rule-system.

Adapting Burns and Flam's theory to industrial relations in Sweden, we can see the labor market rule-regime as a mixture of formal laws, agreements and informal customs. There has been an interest in the regulation of negotiation procedures for a long time. Early examples are the laws of the Labor Court and of the Collective Agreement, the December-compromise between SAF and LO in 1906, and the Saltsjöbaden Agreement from 1938.

Burns and Flam's theory of rule regimes and social interaction has to be specified in defined institutionalized contexts. The analysis of collective bargaining should be anchored in concrete reality, rather than reduced to the abstractions of, for example, game-theory. It is also essential to avoid being drowned by the many details of the negotiation processes. Some structure is needed to sort the facts of negotiations so that they can be confronted with the theoretical structures we try to apply to them.

Anselm Strauss (1978) has presented a specific research strategy for negotiation research. He points out four important levels of analysis: 1) There are *structural contexts* within which negotiations occur. 2) For each negotiation there is subsequently a set of *structural properties*. 3) Each negotiation occurs in a *negotiation context*, these are the conditions applying to the specific negotiation. 4) Finally in the negotiation process the actors are involved in *sub-processes of negotiations*. These are for example making compromises, paying debts, reaching agreements etc.

Strauss suggest that his research strategy can sensitize researchers to possibilities in their data, it can be used to compare different negotiations, to discover the contextual properties of negotiations which are salient for the specific material, and as a predictive guide.

Strauss's research strategy can be compared to the different levels of analysis in Burns and Flam's multi level model of social systems. The structural context can be compared to Burns and Flam's macro level where we find institutions and cultural formations which structure and regulate interaction. Strauss's structural properties can be compared with the aggregate effects and patterns which can be found on the macro-level in Burns and Flam's analysis. Strauss's negotiation context and sub-processes of negotiations are what Burns and Flam calls meso-level phenomena. Here we find the concrete interaction settings and games, the specific rules and procedures which govern wage negotiations, the particular interaction opportunities and constraints, and the reward and cost structures in the concrete negotiation setting.

In this study, I have tried to focus on structural contexts, the structural properties of negotiations and the negotiation context, that is, focusing on the macro and meso level, leaving the sub-processes of negotiations to others.

Taking the Swedish wage negotiation system as an example; the *structural context* at the macro level consists of the established social relations between the different labor and employers organizations, the relations between the organizations and the state, economic conditions, and the historical background to the wage negotiation system. In chapter two, I will describe these properties of the Swedish WNS.

The structural context specifies certain *structural properties* of the wage negotiation system. The state has enacted laws which govern the strike and lockout procedures, and mediation. The fact that the unions have started to compete with each other has created a situation in which each union is trying to safeguard itself from the advances of other unions. On another level, economic conditions exert a great influence over the bargaining power of the parties.

The *negotiation context* at the meso-level is the conditions prevailing in one specific negotiation. A specific union has its particular allies and opponents at that moment. It has a counterpart with specific orientations and strategies. The purpose of the negotiation can be overt or covert (such as organizational-political maneuvers). The economic conditions facing each negotiation may be different. In chapter three, I will in more detail describe the negotiation content which surrounded the dramatic transformation of the Swedish WNS between 1980 and 1986.

*Sub-processes of negotiation* consist of tactical action and strategic planning, the social interaction in the negotiation process. Other sub-processes are the internal negotiations which may occur between members of organizations and their negotiating representatives.

Having so outlined the properties of rule-governed negotiation systems, the negotiations themselves have to be investigated. A number of concepts are important in the understanding of the negotiation process. These will be expounded in the following section.

## The Negotiation process

In the wage negotiation process, actors negotiate within the limits which the rule regime places on the negotiation system. They may adhere to the rules or break them, but action is always taken bearing the rule regime in account. Not anybody is an actor in such a process. The actors in a negotiation situation are the controllers of resources which are placed at their disposal, they have intentions which may be their own or the intentions of those who they represent, and they act and interact in their negotiations. At the same time, they participate in the structuring and restructuring of the rule-regime, organizing and regulating the negotiations. The negotiations lead to outcomes which are evaluated by the actors and which are compared with the intentions at the outset.

Competing groups have different amounts and qualities of power resources. The properties of these resources define to some extent the logic of the situation. For example, Korpi's power-balance model shows how differences in power resources contribute to the probability of conflict between the actors.[16] Actors meet with their power resources in negotiations. It is in this meeting that intentions have to be translated into outcomes. An actor can be said to have exercised power if he is able to translate his intentions into favorable outcomes.

The rule regime governs the system! This means that there are rules of behavior which to some extent define the situation, the agents, and the actions which are legitimate. These rules can be changed by the actors in the course of their interactions.

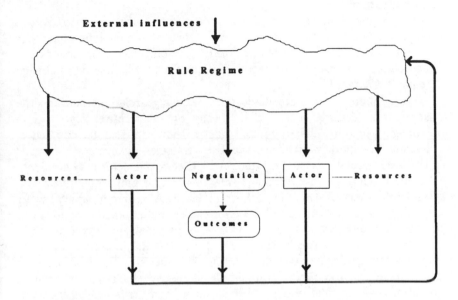

Figure 1.2: A model of a negotiation system

A negotiation is a social interaction between two or more persons or actors. Each actor hopes to obtain something from the other, commodities, favors, information, or some other value. The actor can achieve this through trading something he has got which the other actor desires.

In the negotiation process each actor uses his resources to induce concessions from the other actor. Each actor has certain conceptions about himself, about others and about his desires and goals. The purpose of negotiation is to change these perceptions of the other actor in order to make him believe it is desirable to close a deal. In other words: act tactically in Stevens (1963) terms.

The negotiation process can be visualized as Thibaut and Kelly (1959) do, as a series of matrices where each actor's action, combined with the other actor's action, will produce a result with a specific value for each actor. The result can be positive, that is rewarding, or it can be negative, that is experienced as a cost.

The matrix of possible actions and outcomes (i.e. the pay-off matrix) represents the subjective conception and evaluation by each actor of the negotiation context. This matrix is partly the result of the structuring and restructuring of the actor's model of reality, his goals, expectations, and action alternatives.[17]

In a negotiation, an actor tries to influence the other actor to act in a way that is favorable for him. This is done through manipulating the other actors conception of the context, either the pay-offs or possible actions and interactions. The essence of negotiation can thus be said to be to change the pay-off matrix.[18]

Negotiation systems are made up of exchange relations between the participating actors. These relations can be cooperative, entailing an exchange which results in mutual gains. They can also be conflictive, meaning that both parties use punitive strategies against each other.[19] Finally these relations can be exploitative, that is, one actor may dominate the other. The fact that exchange relations can be both cooperative and conflictive inserts a dynamic in these relations. A setting in which two or more actors participate with both cooperative and conflictive actions can be called a mixed-motive game. This involves a certain degree of complexity in the game. The logic of conflict dictates certain actions and strategies, while the logic of cooperation suggests other courses of action.

A negotiation system continually develops and changes. The changes occur as consequences of negotiations over substantive issues, as effects of intended action, or as a result of strategic maneuvering or negotiation about the structural properties of the negotiation system. I will in chapter two study the development and change of the Swedish WNS.

A negotiation system is an ongoing, unsolved conflict. If the conflict had been resolved, only one specific rule would be needed to distribute the resource or value which earlier was negotiated about. The fact that there are negotiations indicates that there still is a conflict of interest. Further, this indicates that it might be in the interest of each party to change the negotiation system in a way which would promote their own interest. But since each actor is likely to experience opposition from the other party, such maneuvering might lead to counter-strategies which eventually destabilize the system.

The actors in a negotiation system may be collective bodies (delegations) or they may be representatives. The latter leads to the possibility of a distancing between the representative and his constituency.

From the constituency's side there develops a problem over the ability to bring substantive issues up to the negotiation table. From the representative's side there arises a problem of legitimacy. Can he count on the support of the members, do they acknowledge him as their legitimate representative and negotiator? The success and survival of the negotiating body, the organization, depends on its ability to produce results for its constituency. The question of the reproduction of the organization can be treated as the problem of providing results for its members. As long as people feel that the organization provides something necessary for them, there will be a good chance for the reproduction of the organization.

*Organizational politics* are the strategies and tactical actions taken by the organization to promote its reproduction through guarding its borders to other organizations at the same time as it tries to enlarge its constituency. A central feature of organizational politics is the maintenance of the organization as an operating and negotiating organization. Organizations develop vested interests which have to be defended.

I suggest that unions are to be seen as political organizations operating in an economic environment.[20] This means that while unions are not unaffected by changing economic conditions, these conditions will affect union behavior only when they motivate groups within the union to pressure the leadership to act in a certain way. I will argue in chapter four that economic changes which make the company more vulnerable to work stoppages generate a political pressure within unions and work groups which results in demands for increased wages.

I assume that opinions, sentiments, and organized pressures within unions evolve into principles of distributive justice which are advanced in negotiations with the employer side. These principles are important for the formation of a collective identity, at the same time as they may be contested by some fractions within the union. The leadership within the union must reconcile these differences and act in a way which secures the survival and growth of the union.

One can identify at least three sources of pressure for change in negotiation systems. Change can be initiated through the social action based on the actors own initiative, by the effects of exogenous forces and pressures, and through endogenous 'forces' i.e. unintended consequences.[21]

Possibly the most important source of change is actor initiated change. Actors learn, change their preferences, alter themselves, gain knowledge and develop their resources and strategies. These new preconditions often lead them to try to alter the negotiation system. The negotiation processes create outcomes which are not intended or foreseen, and this motivates actors to change the system. There are also exogenous factors which affect the distribution of resources, opportunities and outcomes. Actors are the mediating agents bringing about change in response to external events and developments.

## The Wage Negotiation System

The WNS is one of the main arenas for class-conflict in modern capitalist societies. At the same time it is also a manifestation of cooperation between the classes. The distribution of wages and profits is determined in the WNS. Decisions in the WNS affect the economic policy of the country, the international competitiveness of its industry, the level of employment and much more. There are two main processes in the WNS. First there is a basic struggle between employers and employees, or their organizations, based on the power resources each has and can use to punish or reward the other. Secondly there is a societal game, a meta struggle, in which the actors try to restructure the conditions for the basic struggle, In other words, to change the system. This is done through creating and changing institutions, and through making coalitions. (In chapter two, I will in more detail describe the way the different actors  have formed the Swedish WNS.)

The system consists of several actors on different levels. It is not an isolated system, on the contrary, it is connected to political processes in the society, and to the national and international economy. (In chapter three, the features of the present Swedish WNS will be discussed.)

The conditions for the basic struggle vary for different levels of the WNS and for different sectors of the WNS. The goals of the actors at central levels can be quite different from the goals of local actors. On the local or branch level, conditions may vary from branch to branch and from company to company as we shall see in later chapters.

In the basic struggle, the outcome depends a lot on the resources each actor has at his disposal. Resources valuable in this context are those which can be used to punish or reward the other actor. However the outcome does not necessarily depend on the use of these resources.

The aim of negotiations is to achieve an agreement which is experienced by both parties as more beneficial than what could result from an open confrontation. This means that conflict is a most important precondition for an agreement. It is the threat of a conflict which makes an agreement attractive. The alternative situation would enable the stronger actor unilaterally imposing his will on the weaker actor, without a risk of conflict.

In the case of industrial conflict, the nature of the power resources controlled by workers and by employers differ. Employers control capital while the employee only controls his time, which he can sell as labor power. Korpi (1983) describes the differences between capital and labor in regard to power resources as follows:

> As power resources, capital and the means of production have a large domain, wide scope and high concentration potential, as well as high scarcity and convertability. The costs involved in mobilizing and using these resources are relatively low. Furthermore, control over the means of production has high centrality, since it affects people's livelihood. Capital is also typically used to initiate action.

> When regarded as a power resource, human capital is characterized by serious limitations. Usually it has a fairly small domain and narrow scope. Since everybody has some of it, human capital is generally not a highly scarce resource. Where labour power is offered on the labour market, its value depends on demand from capital, and its ability to initiate action is limited. Human capital has low convertability and a low concentration potential. In an era of mass education, formal training beyond a certain level can at times yield diminishing returns. To be effective, the human capital of various individuals and groups must therefore be coordinated on a broad basis. This requires investments in organizations for collective action and hence fairly large mobilization costs.[22]

In the basic struggle strikes or lockouts have different effects on employers and employees. An employee is deprived of his livelihood and therefore is in need of immediate support. He must also rely on the solidarity of his fellow workers. An employer is quite differently affected. If business is slow, the effects of a shutdown may be negligible.[23] On the other hand, if demand is high, the employer may lose not only high profits, but also market shares (which in the long run is more serious). The effect of the use of power resources may thus vary according to the context.

As I will show in chapter two, the actors in the Swedish WNS try to increase their ability to withstand a long conflict by building up funds for the support of their members. They also try to widen the span of their organizations in order to make their conflict measures more effective. In the basic struggle, their power resources can be identified as funds for support of members engaged in conflict, and their degree of organization. The effect these resources have may vary due to the context. The contextual circumstances are opportunities which can be capitalized upon.

The conflicts may have various impacts on the rest of society. These effects constitute a disruptive potential. A combination of a high risk of conflict and a high disruptive potential creates a threatening situation for the society and may serve as a motive for state intervention in the WNS. The desire to control this disruptive potential based on the power resources of the actors, is one of the main reasons behind attempts to structure the WNS. A situation of high disruptive potential and low risk of conflict may make negotiations more difficult and therefore motivate a change in the WNS.

Another important source of change is the development of outcomes. As we suggested earlier, the survival of an organization may depend on its ability to provide results, that is, favorable outcomes, for its members. If favorable outcomes fail to materialize or there are important unintended outcomes, this means that the actor's power decreases and that he will find it harder to legitimize his existence as a representative for the members of the organization. The actor has then to choose between either finding new ways to obtain the favorable outcome, eventually through restructuring the system, or he must define other goals which are within reach.

Outcomes may change as a result of internal developments. If the number of actors increases, this can lead to a decrease in each actor's power, that is, his ability to affect outcomes diminishes. The strategic maneuvering of actors may decrease the ability of each actor to obtain favorable outcomes. Outcomes may change due to external causes. The oil-crisis and the deep recession thereafter resulting in a combination of both stagnation and inflation, made it difficult for both unions and employers to sustain their expectation levels for wages and profits respectively. Both real wages and profits suffered. Outcomes may be affected by other actors. The state can intervene and change its economic policy. The state can also change rules governing the WNS. Examples of this kind of intervention are the creation of the labor court and the laws around collective agreements.

In Sweden, negotiations take place at several levels, central, branch and local levels. The actions at one level may contradict the actions at other levels. An example is the contradiction between solidaristic wage policy at the central level and wage drift processes at the local level. Such contradictions may motivate actors at different levels to try to change the system.

The WNS is at the same time both a structure and a process. It is a structure in the sense that its institutions pose restrictions on the degree of freedom the actors have for their actions. At the same time the WNS is a process. It is through reoccurring activities, the negotiation processes, that the structure is reproduced and modified. As the processes change, the structure also changes, and vice versa. The question of structure and process is not a one-way causal link. A structure is always a precondition in any action situation, but agents act intentionally to change the structure, trying to transform the game they are playing. There are not only structures, but there are also processes of structuration.[24]

# Conclusions

In this chapter I have presented some of the concepts and principles of industrial relations research. The theory of social rule systems allows us to specify and analyze the specific social organization and rule following as well as creative social actors. The theory of social rule systems makes it possible to partially bridge social action and social structure without presupposing normative consensus, and to explain the transition from one social system or institutional framework to another.[25]

The theoretical starting point for this study is that negotiations are made up of exchange relations in which actors use their power resources to both gain materially in the negotiations as well as to restructure the system in a way which they believe benefits their interest. Nevertheless, a negotiation system may develop on its own as the unintended consequences of negotiations and external changes influence it.

Unions are seen as political actors in an economic arena. This does not mean that unions are not subject to the laws of economics, but that these influences must often take the form of membership pressure on the union leadership.

Conceptions of distributive justice may be an important factor forming opinions of both membership and leaders. These principles are essential for the formation of a collective identity which is important for the survival and growth of unions as organizations.

The wage negotiation system is an exchange relationship between a number of actors who act purposely within the constraints of a rule regime which at the same time they may be trying to change. The WNS is the arena where the distribution between 'profits' and 'wages' is decided. The struggle between the actors is based on the possession of power resources which are qualitatively different, labor's being more costly/difficult to mobilize. In chapter four, actors involved in local negotiations are analyzed in terms of their vulnerability to conflict action on the part of the other.

In the following chapters the general framework presented here is used to ask questions and to guide the development of theories and models.

# 2 The Swedish Model

## Introduction

Conflict and struggle, to varying degrees, are endemic to capitalist societies.[26] Institutions have been established and developed in order to structure and regulate conflicts between capital and labor. This institutionalization of conflict - and the establishment of conflict resolution mechanisms - takes the form of particular rule regimes: labor legislation, collective bargaining, mediation and arbitration boards and procedures, collective agreements, and grievance procedures.

Collective bargaining, in particular, is governed by certain regimes. The organizing principles and rules specify, among other things: the ways in which wage negotiations are to be organized and conducted; whether centrally, branch-wise, or locally; the issues other than wages which may be legitimately negotiated in bargaining processes (or those strictly forbidden); and the possible linkages between issues, for example between wages, work rules, and productivity measures.

One characteristic feature of capitalism is its periodic destabilization and restructuring.[27] This chapter focuses on collective bargaining as one institutional area in which to examine certain destabilizing forces and the agents and social games involved in system restructuring. The study points up:

(i)     the interplay between established rule regimes and concrete socio-economic developments: the transformation of the economy, shifts in strategic functions, the relative decline of industry and the emergence of the service economy, the growth in power of private and public white-collar groups associated with the transformation of the economy, and the societal struggle over income distribution in an economy which is stagnating as well as undergoing transformation.

(ii)    social conflict and the exercise of (meta-)power in connection with efforts to structure and restructure social rule systems organizing and regulating particular economic processes and transactions, in this case collective bargaining and wage determination.

Collective bargaining is something more than a rule-governed exchange between two parties, be it in economic or other terms. Flanders (1969) has stressed that even though a collective agreement may be called a collective bargain and it may have the legal status of a collective contract, it does not commit anyone to sell or buy labor. The collective agreement is meant to ensure that whenever a transaction does take place in the labor market, it will take place according to the provisions of the agreement. These provisions are a set of rules intended to regulate the terms of employment contracts. Collective bargaining is thus in its essence a rule-making process. The effect of the negotiation of collective agreements is to impose certain limits on the freedom of actors in the labor market , without extinguishing their freedom.[28]

Based on the power resources at their disposal, the actors join in negotiations to shape and invent new rules. The rules are jointly determined by representatives of employers and employees who share responsibility for their contents and observance, often with legal underpinnings. Collective bargaining is thus analyzable not only in terms of its economic consequences, but also as a process of 'private politics', a rule-making process which resides outside parliament. It follows that a union may be as interested in establishing its rights and action capabilities vis a vis employers as in achieving immediate material gains.

I examine the structural formation and reformation of the Swedish wage bargaining system, particularly 'The Swedish Model' of centralized wage negotiation and administration. The theoretical-methodological focus is on identifying several key organizing principles which give the system its identifying properties and stability, at the same time that institutional failures of, and emerging struggles around, established principles destabilize the system and set the stage for transition to other systems. I periodize the time frame since the Second World War on the basis of characteristic organizing principles prevailing in each period. This provides a point of departure for the systematic comparative analysis of the different systems in the various periods in terms of key performance variables.

This discussion points out that a dominant coalition of employers and blue-collar union representatives, backed by Social Democratic governments, were instrumental in establishing the regime of centralized negotiations which ultimately became known as 'The Swedish Model'. The discussion also considers some of the challenges to it from within and from outside the system. During much of the post-World War Two period, the coalition of representatives of industrialists and industrial blue-collar unions dominated other interests, such as white-collar unions in the private sector, public sector employer and employee representatives, and local unions.

Since the mid-1960s, however, the power of the dominant coalition has been eroded - and the Swedish Model which it had established and maintained was destabilized - by changes in the organization of the Swedish economy, the formation of a comprehensive welfare state, the growth of large white-collar labor collectives (highly unionized) and intensified competition between employee collectives, particularly between white-collar and blue-collar groups. Formal and informal organizing principles and rules were changed. Struggles are currently going on about the future organization of the system.

As we have seen in the previous chapter, each negotiation regime entails identifiable organizing principles and rules. For instance, there are explicit or implicit rules concerning which actors are included in bargaining (and those excluded). In the Swedish context, blue collar unions outside LO and companies outside SAF are excluded from negotiation activities, not to speak of 'syndicalist' and other radical groups. A regime also defines certain issues as 'legitimate'. In Sweden, wages and employment conditions, including fringe benefits, are legitimate issues. Management prerogatives were, until the 1970s, non-negotiable. Finally, certain principles govern the institutionalized strategies to ensure internal discipline in the ranks of the employers' association and the central blue-collar union (LO). Moreover, each party supports the other to a greater or lesser extent in maintaining internal discipline. This has been done, in part, by refusing to negotiate with, or to generally deal with, 'deviant' members.

In the post-war period four major negotiation regimes can be identified. In the following subsections, I shall examine and provide a brief historical description and analysis of the formation and reformation of a few major features of these regimes, and the social agents and struggles involved in their development. Later, I shall briefly examine the performance characteristics of the four major negotiation regimes, as observable in patterns of wage formation and industrial conflict.

The border between sociological and historical studies is to some degree fluid. In this chapter, the narrative spans a period of one hundred years. My ambition has not been to present a new set of data about the Swedish WNS, but to interpret existing data in somewhat different ways. I have therefore relied heavily on secondary sources. The main sources for factual data have been works such as Westerståhl (1945), Hadenius (1976) and Martin (1984). I have also collected background material from the organizations. The labor market organizations usually present chronicles for the wage rounds such as LO (1984). There are also a number of books which have been published after dramatic wage-rounds, such as Nycander (1972). Through the use of different sources, it has been possible to cross-check the data.

My perspective is necessarily that of an outsider. Although the labor-market organizations have been cooperative, it has not been feasible for this research to make use of the archives of the organizations. One reason is the contemporariness of the research effort. Since I am studying what goes on here and now, the organizations' own notes and protocols have not aged enough to loose their confidential nature.

When using organizational material a certain sense of precaution is needed. Handling information is one of the tasks of the organizations I have been studying. The organizations may want to interpret their history in terms which are relevant to the present negotiation situation.

## The Actors in the present WNS

The actors in the WNS are divided into groups depending on the sector of the economy in which they operate. First there is the private sector of the economy, secondly the public sector, which can be divided into munici-palities and the state. Within these sectors, unions are organized into cartels and peak organizations.[29]

The great dividing line between unions is what sector of the economy they operate in. There are also different bargaining cartels for private employees, state employees and municipal employees. In the system as it operated until 1983, peak organizations exercised a considerable influence over their member organizations.

Another dividing line between different organizations is whether they organize blue- or white-collar workers,[30] Within the different unions, the organizational principle differs, some are organized on an industrial basis, while others are organized on an occupational basis. When a union is organized on an occupational basis, employees with the same occupation belong to the same organization, while being organized on an industrial basis means that all employees within an industry or a branch of the economy belong to the same organization.

Some of the important *negotiating actors* in the central arena are: LO, PTK, SAF, in the private sector sector. (There are also a number of other organizations such as SFO, KFO, TA, and KAB).[31] In the public sector on the union side we find aggregations of blue-collar workers (SF and SKAF both in LO) working for the state and the municipalities. The white-collar workers are represented by TCO unions either in the state or the municipal sector; in addition there are SACO unions representing university graduates. On the employers side, SAV is the state employers negotiation body, Kommunförbundet is an association of local municipalities while Landstingsförbundet is an association of county councils. Negotiations in the 1980s are characterized by decentralized negotiations at the industrial branch level. Here we have a number of unions such as Metall, SIF, CF, Fabriks etc., and a number of employers organizations such as VF, JBF etc.

Wage negotiations are directly dependent on the economic and political developments in a country. *Non-negotiating actors* which are influential here are both parliament and government. The government's economic policy is a starting point for negotiations, the government influences the results of negotiations: the income distribution. Parliament has its particular role through its power to make laws and decide on taxes and other charges.

The government is involved in other negotiations which affect income distribution: agricultural negotiations decide to what extent farmers' claims for increased income should be allowed to result in higher food prices or if they are to be accommodated through granting farmers subsidies. Political decisions about child allowances, pensions, health insurance and employers' fees all change the preconditions for wage negotiations. Taxes and prices of public utilities affect the rate of inflation.

There are also a number of *hidden actors*. Various industrial organizations, union coordination committees and the press, influence the wage negotiations. It is important at the end of negotiations that the union officials feel that they have the support of their members. In decisive moments it is of greatest importance to the union that SAF believes that the union can get its members out on a strike. The union members are influenced by the information which is spread about the condition of the Swedish economy and the competitiveness of Swedish industry. When the press discusses these conditions, it can influence the willingness of the union members to strike. The way information is handled is therefore important in wage negotiations.

## The System

There are multiple negotiations going on in the Swedish wage negotiation system: those between employers' organizations such as SAF,

Kommunförbundet, Landstingsförbundet and SAV, and different unions and cartels of unions. These negotiations can be divided into two segments. (Segment being a wider concept than sector, this is to indicate that the conditions and rules are different and the actors have different strategies in the different segments). The segments of Swedish wage negotiations are the public and the private segment.

Negotiations are carried out on three levels in the system. In the private segment the procedure has been until 1983 as follows:

1.  Central negotiations were predominant between 1956 and 1981. These were conducted between the peak organizations: SAF, LO, PTK, and others. The wage levels agreed upon determined the wage increases at the next level.

2.  Industry level negotiations follow the central negotiations. These negotiations are carried out by the unions and their employer association counterparts. The importance of these negotiations varied between different areas. For workers, they are decisive for the distribution of kitties[32] and for solving questions specific for the industry. For white-collar workers the importance has been smaller. In 1983 the pattern was broken when SIF, SALF and CF negotiated at the industry level with VF. Metall also negotiated with VF, JF, Allmänna gruppen and Motor. In the 1984 wage round, industry level negotiations were to dominate the scene.

3.  Local negotiations have been conducted between the companies and the local unions. In the local negotiations, industry level agreements are applied both as regards the amount and the distribution of pay increases. To the degree that actual wage increases are larger than the agreed amount, wage drift is created. Wage drift has been an indeterminate factor in the wage negotiation system. It has been the aim of most unions to compensate for blue-collar workers' wage drift through the implementation of wage development guarantees which formally connected their wage drift to the wage drift of blue-collar workers.

The present system has its roots in the turbulent industrial relations at the turn of the century. The historical roots of the present system will be discussed in the following section.

# The decentralized system: A historical sketch

In Sweden the first association of blue-collar workers was founded in the mid-nineteenth century by skilled workers employed in small manufacturing enterprises.[33] Later during the 1880s, more militant unions were formed which were aimed more at countervailing the power of employers. During this period the Social Democratic movement developed and came to be closely associated with the rising unions.

In 1898 the 'Landsorganisationen' (LO) was constituted. It was from the start a defensive institution with a mandate to support unions which were facing lockout by employers. It had no mandate to support union strike initiatives.[34] This principle guided the strategic behavior of LO until World War II. The major strike and lockout of 1909 reinforced the principle (see later discussions). An offensive LO would have been too vulnerable to large lockouts - a major strategy pursued by the employers' organization at this time to destroy unions. Instead, the national industrial (sector based) unions held the initiative. These unions aimed in general at controlling the numerous, spontaneous strikes which occurred. Such strikes were often ineffective. At the same time, there were various good grounds - and numerous occasions - for industrial disputes. Until 1905 the employers made every effort to undermine unions and collective agreements. The high level of conflict in this formative period of the Swedish wage negotiation system was the result of union organization, the establishment of strike funds, the development of militant strategies, the growth of union solidarity, and other social power developments in connection with the emergence of the labor movement.

Already in 1906 SAF, the Swedish Employers' Association, and LO concluded the 'December Compromise'.[35] SAF's policy at this time, as opposed to some employers who tried, without success, to break unions, was to recognize to a certain extent the rights to organize and negotiate but to insist on management's rights to manage. In exchange for recognizing the unions, SAF required its own affiliates to include a clause in all collective agreements affirming the principle of management prerogatives.[36]

The rising power of the unions seriously challenged the dominance of the employers.[37] On two occasions in the first quarter of the twentieth century, major industrial conflicts took place. The 'great strike of 1909' resulted in a serious setback for the unions, LO losing half its members. In the following years there was a marked decline in the number and scope of industrial disputes. Sixteen years later, on the other hand, the 'great lockout of 1925' was a failure for the employers, demonstrating that the lock-out weapon was no longer a decisive weapon. Over 117,000 workers were locked out, compared to 71,000 in 1909. The employers drew the conclusion that it was no longer feasible to crush or seriously weaken the labor movement as they had almost succeeded in doing in 1909.[38]

During the 1930s, the Social Democratic government, SAF and LO found the time opportune to establish and formalize a rule regime for industrial relations and collective bargaining. On the one hand, employers had failed, as mentioned above, to counter the growth and power of the union movement with the militant strategy of threatening and utilizing the lockout weapon. On the other hand, LO had up to this time played an entirely defensive role. It had little interest in centralized negotiations due to the threat of SAF lockouts. Nevertheless, by now the Swedish labor movement was relatively well established. Its political party, SAP, was the major force in a coalition government (with the agrarian party). The time was ripe for a shift in the principles organizing industrial relations, particularly LO's and SAF's roles. Also, the Social Democratic government was particularly interested in a new rule regime for industrial unions since its economic crises policy was threatened by industrial instability in several sectors. And, of course, international uncertainties and threats during the 1930s reinforced the sense that 'a new order' should be established.

The result was the 'Basic agreement of 1938' (The Saltsjöbaden Agreement). This agreement between LO and SAF established an entire complex of rules and procedures for negotiations: rules to regulate strikes and lockouts, rules governing the annulment of agreements, and rules for dealing with conflicts at companies of particular 'societal importance'. The agreement also established a labor market committee consisting of LO, SAF and neutral representatives. This committee had the responsibility of interpreting and enforcing the agreement.[39]

The Saltsjöbaden agreement not only institutionalized conflict and conflict regulation, but institutionalized the division of power between employers and unions. Owners and managers were to continue to dominate management and production decisions, while workers could associate in labor unions and negotiate about wages and work conditions.

The Saltsjöbaden agreement did not change the role of LO in wage negotiations. The latter continued to be handled by the national unions and their locals. Nevertheless, even in the absence of central administration, normative principles were established which had a global organizing and coordinating effect, in particular the stress placed on 'cooperation' and 'negotiation' rather than on confrontation. (The shift in normative climate was reflected in the substantial decline in the incidence of industrial conflict and in working days lost due to industrial conflict.) In addition, there were a number of 'informal rules' which for decades played a strategic role in the organization of collective bargaining processes. For instance, from 1931 a 'priority rule' was established which made the Swedish metal workers' union (Metall), the largest and most powerful union in LO, the front-runner and wage norm setter in negotiations.[40]

During the Second World War the labor unions and employers' associations were bound, as in many other countries, by a frame agreement. After the war, these agreements were terminated and the labor market agents returned to the pre-war arrangements of independent negotiations.

In 1946 LO recommended to its unions that they try to raise their wages substantially. The result was a relatively large increase of 15 percent and a threat of accelerating inflation. Therefore in 1947 (in agreement with the Social Democratic government), LO advised its member unions to show restraint. However, the average wage increase was 10 percent, viewed by the government as excessive. The government then urged LO to accept a wage-freeze. LO and its membership complied, simply extending the old wage agreement for another year. The following year the Social Democratic government wished to repeat the procedure. LO agreed but wanted to show special consideration for groups which had lagged behind. It turned out that so many special exemptions had to be made that the agreement would have been impossible to manage. Therefore, LO agreed to extend the 1947 agreement for yet another year. After two extensions of the agreement, LO was compelled in 1950 to release the accumulated demands for wage increases. The negotiations resulted in a wage increase of 23 percent![41]

The decentralized system proved unable to effectively regulate wage negotiations and developments. This was, in part, because it allowed only two extreme responses: 'stop' and 'go'. The obvious weaknesses of such an arrangement in a small, open economy were a major motivation behind the formation of what became known as the Swedish Model.

## The Swedish Model of Centralized Negotiations

In preparation for the 1952 negotiations, LO attempted to coordinate the various branch negotiations, allowing some exceptions from a general agreement for those unions with claims for disadvantaged groups of workers. The powerful metal workers' union and the building workers' union were skeptical. They and a number of other unions wanted to advance and negotiate their own claims. In the end, LO was only trusted with the task of negotiating an index agreement with SAF. SAF, however, demanded centralized negotiations in exchange for an index agreement. Only five LO unions (out of 44) were opposed to such centralized negotiations. Ultimately, SAF's proposal prevailed, imposing a new structure on wage negotiations at least temporarily.[42]

The economy was sluggish in 1953 and 1954 so the Social Democratic government felt no need to press LO on wage restraint. In 1955 the economy picked up and prospects for wage increases in 1956 suggested that the government's stabilization policy would be in serious trouble. Already in 1955 LO had felt that centralized wage negotiations would be desirable for 1956 and, indeed, a central contract was signed with SAF.[43]

In 1957 LO informed SAF that they could not participate in centralized negotiations. Instead, independent union negotiations were initiated. These gave meager results, only fractions of a percent. LO was compelled to try to negotiate with SAF and, eventually, signed a two-year agreement. According to the newly promoted chairman of LO, Arne Geijer, SAF was responsible for the initiative to establish central negotiations. SAF managed to close the ranks of its members and maintain a united front against the unions, particularly those unions such as Metall and construction workers who were somewhat opposed to central negotiations. SAF tactics succeeded in making clear to LO and its member unions that their best alternative was to support central negotiations. This was the backdrop for the 25 years of centralized negotiations between LO and SAF for the private sector.[44]

The central white-collar union, TCO (White-collar Union Central Organization corresponding to the all blue-collar LO), was included initially in the attempts to organize central negotiations. This cooperation fell through because of LO's adherence to a principle of combined Kronor/percentage increases in contract formulation, whereas the white-collar unions would only accept percentage forms (since the latter maintain wage and income differentials, an important goal for white-collar unions in regard to white-collar/blue-collar income relations).[45] The Swedish industrial white-collar union  (SIF) signed central agreements with SAF in 1952 and in 1956, under the auspices of TCO. Since 1957, SIF and SAF negotiated centrally. Later (from 1969) a central cartel of private white-collar workers (ISAM - eventually, PTK, the Private White-collar Union Cartel) negotiated with SAF. Parallel centralization occurred on the public side.

From 1956 until 1966, the negotiations entailed a priority rule. SAF and LO negotiated before all other groups. After they reached an agreement in March or April, the other negotiations commenced. The SAF-LO agreement was a starting point and a norm. This contributed to a uniform wage development for both LO and white-collar groups (TCO). There were, however, large differences among unions in gains from local, unauthorized wage increases in the private sector. Similar differences arose between the private sector and the public sector where the latter did not have opportunities to sign, and to draw benefit from, such local, unauthorized contracts. Eventually rules were negotiated and established assuring compensation to blue-collar and salaried groups for the wage drift of LO groups enjoying unauthorized wage increases.

In sum, the centralized system of collective bargaining consisted during the period 1956-1966 of the following structural features:[46]

(i)   The private labor market peak organizations, LO and SAF, negotiated contracts within an established framework of rules and understandings. These agreements to a greater or lesser extent governed wage levels and structures in the LO/SAF area.

(ii)  The LO enjoyed considerable but not complete control over its member unions and over shop floor negotiations and wage developments. While unofficial strikes were few, unauthorized wage increases ('wage-drift')[47] were a persistent 'problem' during the entire period, often equalling the wage increases of the central agreements (see Table 2.1). Branch unions and locals negotiate unauthorized increases, in part due to pressures from their members to maintain traditional differentials, not taken into account in the central agreements. Employers often went along with these demands, either to avoid trouble with their union locals or to express genuine support for a more differentiated or what was felt to be, locally, a more suitable wage structure.

(iii) SAF was relatively successful in coordinating the employers' associations and in exercising control over individual employers. Nevertheless, SAF's sanctions - warnings, chastisement, and fines - against members' agreements to unauthorized wage increases never succeeded in eliminating the problem. As indicated above, individual employers, in the interest of good management-labor relations, would go along with special 'corrective' or 'compensatory' demands. In many instances, managers would take the initiative themselves in order to ensure adequate recruitment of qualified workers and incentives for increased productivity.[48]

(iv)    Up until the mid-1960s, LO/SAF exercised successful hegemony over the collective bargaining system, Private white-collar negotiations and negotiations in the public sector followed and were guided by norms and developments in the LO/SAF area.

(v)     Informally, a neo-corporatist institutional framework - with labor, capital, and state representatives in consultation and negotiation - prevailed. This provided the structural basis in Sweden for systematic regulation of labor markets and wage formation and, in general, the formulation and implementation of economic policy. However, in the case of Sweden the state operated largely as a silent partner, having functioned largely in the meta-level in facilitating the formation of organizing principles and norms to govern collective bargaining. The interests of the state, as indicated earlier, were in reducing industrial strife and controlling wage development and inflationary pressures.

The Swedish Model was sustained over a long period (until the early 1980s), because two powerful and important agents, SAF and LO as well as key political actors had an interest in maintaining it. LO gained the opportunity to implement its solidaristic wage policy. SAF could moderate wage-increases and settlements and ensure a low level of industrial strife. The Social Democratic government succeeded in its economic policy and stabilization goals.

Elite efforts to maintain the system in the face of countervailing forces are illustrated by the informal rule of not allowing contracts other than the LO-SAF contract to be introduced into negotiations between SAF and splinter groups. SAF signed only 'contingent agreements' with independent unions; similarly, LO forced independent companies (outside of SAF) to sign such contingent agreements. This exemplifies how a participation (or exclusion) rule may be enforced. LO and SAF conspired successfully to restrict entry to the wage-negotiation arena.

While Swedish wage levels were among the highest in the OECD countries, sustained improvements in productivity and high rates of rationalization resulted in competitive relative unit labor costs, at least up until the early 1970s. Sweden's growth in industrial production and gross domestic product (GDP), although not spectacular during the period 1955 to 1970, was considerably better than those of the UK and USA, comparable to those of Germany, Austria, Belgium and Switzerland, and only surpassed by up-and-coming countries such as France, Italy, and of course, Japan. The inflation rate, while not in the low class of Germany and Switzerland, nevertheless was respectable up until 1970. As is generally known, Sweden's unemployment rate has been very low, an achievement which it has sustained until today. This accomplishment, which reflects a serious policy commitment, appears even more noteworthy in view of the poor performance on this score of most other OECD countries.[49]

The Swedish collective bargaining system became a source of pride - and in some other countries with unstable industrial relations, an object of envy. The rate of industrial strife, in contrast to the turbulent 1920s and early 1930s when it was among the highest in Europe, has been one of the lowest in the Western world. This performance was blemished somewhat by the rise in unofficial strikes and the several major strikes which took place in the 1970s and early 1980s, a subject to which we return later (see Table 2.1)

The overall excellent economic performance of Sweden up until the late 1960s cannot be attributed only, or even mainly, to its centralized system of bargaining. Nevertheless, in a society with a powerful labor movement and the highest level of union density, the performance is noteworthy. Certainly, the collective bargaining system contributed to labor market discipline and stability, an essential ingredient in the economic performance of any industrialized country.

## The Swedish Model in Transition

1966 was a momentous year, with several noteworthy developments. A major industrial conflict threatened, but LO and SAF managed to reach an agreement. The agreement gave LO workers a 12 percent increase over three years. included here was 4 percent compensation for reduced working hours. At the same time, the white-collar workers managed to negotiate an increase of 18-20 percent in a three year agreement. This was a challenge to LO, to be followed by further challenges. The LO was particularly critical of the compensation of white-collar workers for the wage-drift of blue-collar workers. Wage-drift reflected tough rationalization in industry, LO argued that white-collar groups should not draw benefits from it, through for instance automatic compensation. Such tensions between blue-collar and white-collar collectives and between the private and public sectors became an increasing threat to the stability of Swedish wage negotiation system and its effectiveness in regulating conflict.[50]

1966 was the first year when white-collar workers employed by the state and local authorities enjoyed the full right to negotiate and to strike. This changed the power base for the publicly employed. It also increased the number of full-fledged negotiating agents and complicated negotiations considerably.

Several innovations in contracts were introduced around this time. A persistent issue in the central negotiations concerned the problem of dealing with industrial branches where workers who did not enjoy opportunities for wage-drift gains expressed discontent. Until 1966, the principal solution had been to try to settle such matters ahead of - and therefore separate from - the main negotiations. Rising discontent and the number of requests for exemptions from the main agreement reached the point where it became very cumbersome negotiation-wise and administratively to continue with such an arrangement.

Ultimately, SAF and LO agreed to introduce a wage development guarantee for its members along with a new clause in the main agreement allowing for higher increases in branches with low wage levels. This arrangement reflected a fundamental understanding between LO and SAF on the principle that a long-term stable wage development was desirable and that this depended in part on a 'fair wage structure'. The new arrangements were to have substantial and unforeseeable impacts later.[51]

The discussion following the negotiations led to a proposal from SAF for a coordination of all negotiations which entailed absolute increases (as opposed to percentage increases). Economic experts were to decide on the total level of such raises. Deductions for wage-drift and other labor costs were to be made to ensure the maintenance of internationally competitive labor costs and investment propensities. The remainder after deductions was to be divided between blue-collar and white-collar collectives.[52]

Both the blue-collar and white-collar central organizations, LO and TCO respectively, rejected the proposal. Instead, SAF, LO and TCO agreed to establish an expert group of leading economists from their organizations to investigate the role of wages and salaries in the economy. The 'EFO-group' (Gösta Edgren, Karl Olof Faxén, and Claes-Erik Odhner) formulated the Scandinavian or EFO model for the Swedish labor market.[53] The rules of the model determined an available economic latitude for wage increases in the private sector based on growth in productivity. The rules for distribution of available income were to be negotiated in collective bargaining. It was understood that the distribution would be carried out, in part, according to the 'solidaristic wage policy', which was pushed by low income unions in LO, in order to improve the income levels and wage differentials of low wage workers. According to the model, public sector collectives would receive increases matching those in the private sector. These matching increases were expected to be inflationary, since they would not be based on corresponding increases in productivity.

Clearly, the model combined the major concerns of the two dominant actors at that time: SAF's interest in limiting wage formation in the private sector to a level consistent with productivity increases and in assuring the leading role of the private sector in wage formation; LO's interest in assuring sustained, and reasonably predictable, real increases for blue-collar workers and at the same time in maintaining its leadership role and the integration of the blue-collar labor movement. This was particularly important vis a vis the low-income unions (such as textile, transport, and retailing), who would be reluctant to accept the wage-restraint discipline imposed by the rules of the EFO model.

After 1967 LO and TCO initiated discussions on the possibilities of coordinating their negotiations. These were aborted when SIF, a major union in TCO, publicly criticized the idea. LO continued to press for greater coordination. Indeed, LO seems to have been the only major agent on the labor market which has had a sustained interest in coordinating negotiations on the labor market as a whole. In 1969 the industrial white-collar union (SIF) along with the foremen's union (SALF) moved to counteract the LO position by signing an early agreement with SAF, that is prior to LO (and Metall).[54]

Upon obtaining the right to strike, white-collar workers in the public sector became an increasingly important factor in the wage determination process. The total number of employees in the public sector substantially increased during this period in connection with the very rapid growth in public expenditures and of the 'welfare state' generally (see Table 2.1)

LO's share of total union memberships dropped from 81 percent in 1950 to 64 percent in 1980 (see table 3.1). This is one of several indicators of LO's loss of dominance in the collective bargaining system. Actors which emerged and increased in importance were public worker unions, public employers' representatives (state and municipalities), and white collar unions in the private as well as public sectors. The latter established large cartels and formulated militant policies. For instance, the white collar unions in the private sector formed a cartel (PTK), which negotiated with SAF. In this complicated setting, LO and SAF were no longer hegemonic. The wage negotiation process became an equation which a sizable group of actors attempted to solve, in the absence of institutions which enable them to directly negotiate and to settle with one another. Instead, labor collectives tended to negotiate with one another indirectly through their employer counterparts.

Several of the new types of negotiation problems and conflicts which emerged in conjunction with these developments were: (a) White-collar workers became more insistent in their demands for compensation for blue-collar workers' wage-drift, on the one hand, whereas LO insisted on compensation for salary merit increases among white-collar workers. A major source of conflict between LO and the private white-collar cartel of unions (PTK) has been the issue of the formula for wage-drift compensation. In 1977 an 80 percent compensation rule (instead of 100 percent) was forced on the white-collar cartel PTK by SAF through threatening a major lock-out. However, the struggle has continued and was a major factor in the breakdown of cooperation between LO and PTK. Along similar lines, Metall tried (1980) to introduce a policy that white-collar workers be laid-off just as blue-collar workers are subject to layoffs under current operating principles. (b) Tensions and disagreements emerged and deepened between the private and public sides of the white-collar workers' movement. (c) There were also increased tensions and conflicts between municipal worker unions and private sector unions within LO over questions of wage-drift. (d) TCO unions and the 'university graduates white-collar unions' (SACO/SR) competed and struggled in the private as well as the public spheres.

At the end of the 1960s and during the 1970s unofficial strikes became an increasing problem (see Table 2.1). By international standards, the strike-wave was minor. However, it was seen as undermining LO's position. The continuation of wage-drift, reaching particularly high levels in some years during this same period, also pointed up the inability of LO and SAF to control their members. Employers reached agreements with local labor unions which violated the spirit, and often enough the letter, of central contracts.

As a result of growing unrest on the labor market, the formal agreement for 1970-1973 provided for very high wage increases. Then in 1973, in reaction to the downward business cycle, LO signed an agreement involving moderate wage increases. As this agreement expired, the business cycle started to turn upward. At the same time the oil-crisis struck. A downturn was expected in Sweden. In this context LO signed a low increase contract for one year. Since business continued to boom, company profits soared and wage-drift jumped markedly.[55]

The exercise of wage restraint became increasingly problematic. The Social Democratic government hoped to establish a new principle for wage negotiations. The basic problem was that the government could only influence the central actors to a very limited degree. These in turn enjoyed only modest influence over their members and wage determination. Local actors continued to generate wage-drift and to contribute to the wage explosion of the mid-1970s. At the same time, the various 'wage development' indexes or guarantees spread wage-drift developments throughout the economy, private as well as public sectors.

Increasingly, the 'question of taxes' became a labor market question. A few white-collar unions, had made this an issue already in the 1960s. But high marginal tax rates in Sweden - which became particularly pronounced in the period around 1970 - made it increasingly difficult for these unions to raise the disposable income of their members (rising inflation was also to play a role in limiting gains in real disposable income). The LO under Arne Geijer opposed linking the tax question to wage and income questions. This agenda rule held until the new LO head, Gunnar Nilsson, came into power in 1971.[56]

It had become obvious to most that taxes had to be brought into the discussion of wages and income, at least in a country with tax rates as high as Sweden's. High marginal tax rates forced up wage increases to ensure maintained or increased after tax real income. The Social Democratic government also realized that it was no longer possible to raise additional tax revenues through income tax. A 'package solution' was attempted during the so-called 'Haga Meetings', 1974-1976, with the participation of the employers, the major central unions and the state. Proposals, initiated by the government, became 'informal agreements' coupling wages and salaries, taxes and unit costs of employees with each other. The new deal entailed reductions in income taxation in exchange for labor unions showing wage restraint. At the same time, the loss of revenue to the state was to be counter-balanced by increases in 'employer fees' (a percent tax on employee income which the employer is obliged to pay the state).[57] These fees increased by 4 percent annually between 1973 and 1977, driving up the unit labor costs of Swedish blue-collar workers and white-collar workers.[58]

Thus, not only did centrally negotiated wages increase substantially in the mid-1970s, but wage-drift and employer fees as well. The result was a dramatic increase in total employee costs (more than 22 percent increase from just 1974 to 1975).[59]

The Swedish model depended on growing income available for wage increases, that is, an expanding economy.[60] Economic growth could be divided between profits, wages and the demands of a growing public sector. This model faced formidable problems when economic stagnation set in and persisted at the same time that the public sector and transfer payments continued to expand. The slowdown in growth transformed what had been a more or less 'positive-sum' game into a 'zero-sum' game.

At the same time, the increase in the number of powerful actors - without an institutional framework to coordinate and regulate the new, destabilizing interactions - contributed to the relative decline of the powers of each actor to influence the wage and salary systems in favorable directions.

In these changed circumstances, the SAF-LO coalition could no longer dominate incomes policy, wage negotiations and wage developments as they had done earlier. New actors with diverse interests and aims were included in the collective bargaining system. The wage formation process developed into a wage-carousel where the demands of one labor union pushed up the demands of others. None of the actors enjoyed sufficient control over the situation to be able either to fulfill its goals or to establish a new system. This situation led to high uncertainty and increasing conflict potential.

In 1980 the unthinkable in Sweden happened. Labor market tensions resulted in a major conflict with more than 20 percent of the labor force on strike or lock-out. The Swedish economy was at a near stand-still for almost two weeks.[61]

A new and uncertain mood set in after 'The Great Conflict'. On the one hand, the general attitude was 'never again'. On the other, some key actors concluded that a new collective bargaining system was needed. The large companies in the engineering branch - Volvo, Electrolux, LM Eriksson, Saab-Scania, Asea, among others - were the most open and assertive about this. They increased their earlier pressures to return more to branch level agreement (and perhaps ultimately to a system where enterprise level negotiations would prevail).

Although negotiations in 1981 followed the normal, centralized pattern, SAF had already decided to act upon the initiative of the Engineering Federation (VF). A change in SAF's statutes was necessary in order to shift to branch level negotiations. This shift was made in 1982, allowing VF to carry through its plan for more decentralized negotiations.

Later, in the course of the 1983 negotiation round, VF signed an agreement with Metall. It also signed an agreement with the white-collar workers union (SIF) in the private sector. The strategy pursued by the federation was similar to that used by SAF in the 1957 negotiations. In this case, however, SAF stalled the central negotiations while VF was allowed to deal directly with Metall. Metall felt that to oppose VF, possibly by striking, in order to maintain centralized negotiations would have been a move very uncertain of success and would have denied them opportunities to settle old claims with VF (which was the carrot that VF offered). Any other response would have been difficult for Metall to justify to its members.

Industry level negotiations between employer federations and labor unions became the dominant pattern in 1984, although LO tried to coordinate the negotiations on its own (that is without support from SAF). The negotiations resulted in high nominal wage increases.

Inflation in Sweden reached one of the highest levels among OECD countries. The Social Democratic government took several initiatives, in particular calling 'national meetings' in 1984 with the participation of the government, unions and employer organizations to discuss questions of wages, income, and economic policy. Vague agreements to adhere to a five percent wage increase ceiling were made. LO, supporting the Social Democratic government's policy, managed with considerable effort - and not without some assistance from the government - to keep its membership within the five percent frame. A major strike of public sector employees was unleashed in May, stopping all air traffic and number of other important services. The strike continued for three weeks and resulted in an agreement above the five percent ceiling (although the public unions viewed the 'excess' as promised compensation for losses the previous year).

## New internal and external problems and conflicts

Swedish industrial relations, and in particular labor-management negotiations, face problems and challenges today which did not exist earlier or were of an altogether different character at the time the Swedish Model was established and functioned more or less effectively.

Some of the major problems and conflicts which have emerged and become more serious over the past 10 to 20 years are:

(i)  The set of economic and political constraints and opportunities within which collective bargaining takes place have been transformed. Above all, major changes have occurred in the macroeconomic and political context:

a) The Swedish economy has become increasingly internationalized, with growth in the size and importance of the export sector; at the same time, the international economy has been, since the early 1970s, turbulent and unstable;

b) There has been economic stagnation since the late 1960s (see 'change in GNP' and 'change in industrial production' in Table

2.1), which has evoked struggles among groups trying to maintain or increase real income levels at one another's expense;

c) An immense welfare state and public sector has been established, with its heavy demands, through taxation, on private income;

d) The problems of achieving economic stabilization in a complex, externally dependent economy have become formidable. Policies and institutional measures which worked relatively well earlier no longer assure stabilization, in part because the problems are to a certain extent international in character and the nation-state, particularly a small one, has great difficulty dealing effectively with them on its own. Also, various government policies, including taxation, and labor market legislation have had a complex, inconsistent impact on wage negotiation processes and on labor markets generally.

(ii) Labor market actors and their relations have been transformed. The major developments here have been

a) The emergence of powerful salaried employee unions and the substantial growth of the public sector, where the latter has quite different 'game rules' and development logic than the private sector (particularly the open, internationalized sectors)

b) The erosion of LO-SAF dominance over collective bargaining and wage development in Sweden.

White-collar workers have established themselves as important actors. This has made the labor movement more heterogeneous. Moreover, there is no intimate linkage between the Social Democratic Party and the white-collar workers' unions corresponding to that between the SPD and the LO.

Important and powerful enterprises, such as Volvo, Electrolux, LM Eriksson, Saab-Scania, as well as the export sector generally, explored new systems of production organization and payment, geared to the demands of their production and markets, particularly export markets, as well as to rapid changes in technology. As a result, these actors became less and less disposed to accept SAF's authority and attempts to impose discipline.

(iii)    New types of tensions, negotiation problems, and conflicts have emerged in connection with the appearance of new actors and relationships. Thus, a collective bargaining system which had been relatively simple, dominated by SAF and LO and their central members, has been restructured by the appearance of new and powerful actors, in particular the salaried employee unions, both on the public and private sides. In general, there has been an intensification of inter-group competition and distributional conflicts. This concerns, above all, struggle among labor union cartels such as LO and the private white-collar cartel (PTK), and public sector unions and private sector unions (these tensions and conflicts are found also within LO).

(iv)    The struggle between the public and private parts of the economy has become more open and systematic. Employers and unions on the private side act in consort to improve wages and salaries in the private sphere relative to the public sphere. And, in turn, public sector unions and/or employers try to counteract or nullify the private sector moves. The public sector unions insist that they want no more but also no less than groups in the private sector. On the other hand, SAF, LO and PTK are in general agreement that manufacturing employees should get more. The public/private struggle concerns not only income distribution and wage differentials, but also questions of initiative, status and power in collective bargaining processes.

(v)    Central-local tensions and conflicts. This is not only a question of wage drift, unofficial strikes, and local tendencies to oppose and to deviate from central agreements and 'income policies'. It also relates to the demands which local organizations and interests make on the central organizations. In some cases these demands relate openly to the freedom to take initiatives and to 'negotiate on their own', as exemplified in the move of the employers of the engineering industry (VF) to decentralize wage negotiations, at least to the branch level. The problem of central-local tensions - not a new phenomenom in the Swedish context - has become more acute over the past 15 years, in part because of the very success of the central incomes policy (that of solidarity) bringing about substantial income compression; and, in part, because of turbulence, uncertainty and failures of economic policy, in the face of global shocks, recession, and inflation.

# Periodization and empirical performance of the Swedish WNS

## Introduction: Four epochs of social organization

In this section I periodize the post-war history of the Swedish wage negotiation system (WNS) into four periods or epochs.[62] These are defined accorrate which opens up alleys of coding to system organizing principles and functioning. This should be stressed: *The epochs are divided according to regime principles and not according to economic criteria. The economic circumstances are of course of great importance, but they provide the setting in which the actors play, they do not determine the logic of the situation.*[63]

Each epoch can then be characterized by a rule regime with certain organizing principles and core rules. The regime associated with an epoch structures fields of action and games relating to wage negotiation: participating actors, rules of the game, legitimate issues and strategies, structures of action opportunities and payoffs. This results in certain observable patterns of performance but also efforts to maintain or reform the particular wage negotiating system. Thus, my analysis of the social organization of the Swedish WNS is combined with quantitative analyses of wage agreements, wage-drift, and industrial conflict rates, among other variables.

In a certain sense, I associate different analytical models with the four epochs, where each epoch is expected to exhibit differing patterns of negotiation and conflict, negotiated outcomes, and wage performance. I want to stress that I am not trying to explain the performance of the Swedish economy during the years encompassed by the four epochs. My aim is a more modest one, concerned with explaining some of the performance characteristics of the wage negotiation system.

In the first epoch (I), the organizing principle of the WNS was decentralized, that is branch specific, union-level negotiations for blue-collar workers. This system was transformed into a system with centralized LO-SAF negotiations, which characterized the second epoch (II). In the transition from epoch II to III, the centralized system with LO-SAF hegemony was transformed into a bi-polar system with centralized private and public negotiations. A dominant game in this period entailed competition between public and private employee collectives, played out through their negotiations with representatives of public and private employers, respectively. At the end of epoch III, the wage negotiation system was transformed further into a multi-polar system, involving complicated income distribution struggles between public and private, blue-and white-collar collectives. While in epoch II LO and SAF could disregard - or settle more on their own terms with - other groups of employees, in the later epochs other collectives had the power to insist on their terms.

The social organizational features of the four epochs are summarized below:

I      **1946-1955.**

The epoch of decentralized, separate branch-level wage negotiations. The period, starting after the Second World War, ended with the establishment of central wage negotiations. During this period LO and SAF had little to say about the conduct of wage negotiations. There was an informal rule prevailing that the Metal-Workers' Union negotiated first and the others followed. The latter had the opportunity to base their demands on the agreement achieved by Metall, the largest and most powerful union. Also, the LO-economists, Rehn and Meidner, argued that the unions should try to get as much as they could when business went well and there was a high demand for labor.

LO was in no position to enforce wage restraint. Systematic restraint could be achieved temporarily only through exhortations of LO and the Social Democratic Government and/or through deflationary policies.

II     **1955-1965.**

The 'Golden Age' of the Swedish Model, with central negotiations and SAF-LO hegemony. SAF and LO in large part dominated the wage negotiation process and outcomes. Their negotiation results served as the norm for the rest of the labor market. Central negotiations between SAF and LO were conducted according to a formula of rules which took into account productivity increases, international and national economic developments (see p. 30 concerning the EFO model). Wage agreements were reached which were in large part consistent with stable economic development.

However, during this period, wage negotiations became more and more difficult, in part because of the large number of exemptions which had to be made in order to assure the cohesiveness of LO (and individual union acceptance of central negotiations).[64] Public and private white-collar unions played no major roles in the wage bargaining processes. Public employees did not have the right to strike and, therefore, were in no position to launch a major challenge to the system. Moreover, both the public and private white-collar employees were organized into several unions which served more as networks and opinion forums than bargaining agents.

Public sector employment grew substantially during the period as a result of the rapid expansion of the welfare state. There was a parallel increase in the number of white-collar employees in the private sector. White-collar workers in both the public and private sectors increasingly joined unions. Nonetheless, only 55 percent of the white-collar workers were organized compared to 90 percent of the blue-collar workers; LO had 3.4 times as many members as the white-collar workers' peak organization (TCO). The latter, in contrast to LO, has never been a bargaining agent or a major political force. Without a doubt LO, with its close informal ties to the Social Democratic Party, was the dominant peak organization on the employee side and a formidable counterpart to SAF, particularly in the context of Social Democratic governments.

III    **1966-1973.**

The decline of SAF-LO hegemony and the establishment of bipolar centralism. There emerged a new central arena, public sector wage bargaining, with powerful new actors, the public sector unions, challenging the dominance of LO and SAF. These unions refused to be governed by several of the principles and formulas governing the earlier epoch.

In 1966 public employees obtained the legal right to strike and quickly became full-fledged negotiation agents. Their unions were eager to settle old scores. For instance, public employees neither benefited directly from wage-drift which many production workers enjoyed, nor did they have guarantees or compensation for wage-drift. Certain categories of employees had fallen substantially behind in their wage development. (Although white-collar workers were presumed not only to have higher status but to enjoy higher incomes than blue-collar workers.) Through a major strike against the school system, teachers achieved major increases in their salaries in 1966.

In 1969 the white-collar unions in the private sector (SIF, SALF and CF) managed to get together for the first time and signed a five year joint agreement with SAF. This signalled the entrance of yet another powerful actor into the Swedish WNS, although a formal cartel was not established until 1973. The long contract period of the agreement proved to be a major liability in the turbulent early 1970s and effectively excluded them until 1973. The private white-collar workers fared worse during this period than they had earlier, relative to blue-collar workers. While the latter received increases on the average of 9.0 percent, the former got only 7.5 percent under their contract terms. (see table 2.1) They were to make up for this initial failure by organizing into a powerful cartel, PTK, and negotiating much more militantly, particularly with an eye on blue-collar developments. This contributed to the formation of an additional central arena.

IV     **1974-1983**

Multi-polar centralism with a set of powerful peak collectives. This period was characterized by multiple arenas at the central level and new forms of coalition formation. LO and SAF no longer dominated wage developments. A new set of actors fully exercised their rights to battle over their share of income. A sustained competition between the public and private sectors of the economy had begun. Differentials between public and private employee collectives became increasingly difficult questions.

More than 70 percent of the white-collar employees in Sweden were by now organized. The private white-collar cartel, PTK, negotiated with SAF for the first time in 1974. Wage competition between blue-and white-collar unions and between private and public sector collectives became fully established. These struggled with one another at the national level over income distribution.

A characteristic feature of the epoch was the preoccupation with complex calculations of differentials and the formulation of complex guarantees (indexation) of relative developments among different collectives. Furthermore, a new type of game emerges where new coalition partners in negotiations were sought. Sometimes LO and PTK negotiated together vis a vis SAF, sometimes not. A constellation of public sector unions, known as the 'gang of four' - an on-and-off-again coalition of blue-collar and white-collar collectives in the public sector - was established to try to enhance their bargaining power and to improve their position relative to the private sector collectives.

These struggles and games gave rise to high uncertainty and serious tensions and threats, leading to strikes in some cases and setting the stage for the 'Great Conflict' of 1980. This also became a period where there were manifest struggles over maintaining, reforming, or transforming the wage negotiation system.

## System performance variables

We have examined a number of quantitative variables which could be expected to be affected by the particular organizing principles, rules of the game, and negotiation procedures of the WNS systems in the different epochs which have been identified. Among the variables examined are wage formation for blue- and white-collar workers, including wage-drift for the former, industrial conflicts including 'wildcat strikes', and the relationship between formal agreements and wage-drift. In addition, organizational data on unionization, employment and other economic indicators are presented.[65] Means and standard deviations (SD) are given for each epoch.

The statistical data in this chapter has been collected from various sources. This introduces the problem of consistency, compatibility and accuracy in the statistical material. I have tried to use as consistent measures as possible. But sometimes it has not been possible. For example: In order to get data for workers wages, I had to combine data from three different sources. The first period also excluding women. I claim that this data is still useful in my analysis.

## Analysis and conclusions

Epoch I, as epoch IV, was a turbulent period with high variance in wage developments, in inflation, in changes in industrial production, and in changes in industrial profits. The international inflation in 1949-1950, in part in connection with the Korean war, spurred this development. Also, central control over performance outcomes and developments was very limited.

The data indicate that during the first period the average blue-collar wage increase was 9.3 percent per year. The variation was enormous, with a minimum of 0 percent (wage freeze) and a maximum of 21.6 percent.

The standard deviation was 6.3. This was a period of stop-go cycles, where the government tried to stabilize the economy with macro-economic policy measures. Wage increases were higher only in the fourth epoch, and the variation in the first period has never been matched since.

Most of the increases occurred in the union branch negotiations which averaged 5 percent. The largest variation was also to be found in these agreements. Still, a large part of the wage increases stemmed from wage-drift. This was on the average 4.2 percent during this epoch, with a standard deviation of 1.4. The average of the ratio of agreement wages to wage-drift was 1.0 with a standard deviation of 0.8.

The performance pattern in Epoch II differs substantially from that of the first Epoch, including the variance in wage-drift (although average wage-drift itself did not differ significantly. This pattern holds for the entire post-war period). Worker wages grew on average by 7.0 percent per year. Compared to the earlier as well as later periods, variance in key performance variables was low. Industrial conflicts, including 'wildcat strikes' were rare.

Economic circumstances during this period were very favorable. GNP growth was on the average 4.2 percent during the period, inflation on the average 3.7 percent. Productivity grew on the average by 4.8 percent, industrial production by 5.7 percent.

Compared to the preceding period, wages grew considerably faster in Epoch III, but variance remained relatively low. Particularly noteworthy was the emergence of a negative correlation between increases in wages through formal central contracts and wage-drift. (In the preceding period the correlation had been close to 0) There was a three-fold increase in the rate of industrial conflict (measured by working-days lost in industrial conflicts), putting it on a level comparable to that found in Epoch I (still very low by international standards).

The economy performed fairly well. GNP grew on the average by 3.4 percent, industry production by 4.4 percent, productivity by 4.4 percent, while inflation was on the average 5.3 percent. The state's finances were sound, public sector employment was growing, so were taxes and payroll taxes (which grew on the average by 1.0 percent a year).

In Epoch IV, the average nominal wage increase was the highest of the four periods. The variation in wage increases was only greater in the first period, which resulted also from a pluralistic negotiation system. Although wage drift varied the most compared to the other epochs, the variation in contract wages is even larger.

Table 2.1a:   System performance variables

| Variables | Epoch | | | |
|---|---|---|---|---|
| | I | II | III | IV |
| | 1946-55 | 1956-65 | 1966-73 | 1974-83 |
| *Blue-collar workers* | Yearly averages | | | |
| Formal contract increases | 5.0% | 3.0% | 4.9% | 5.8% |
| (SD) | (5.1) | (1.1) | (1.7) | (2.6) |
| Wage drift | 4.2% | 4.0% | 4.1% | 4.0% |
| (SD) | (1.4) | (0.9) | (1.1) | (1.8) |
| Total wage increases | 9.3% | 7.0% | 9.0% | 9.8% |
| (SD) | (6.3) | (1.5) | (1.7) | (3.7) |
| Real total wage increases | 5.0% | 3.4% | 3.7% | -0.1% |
| Formal contract / wage drift | 1.0 | 0.8 | 1.3 | 1.7 |
| (SD) | (0.8) | (0.3) | (0.5) | (0.9) |
| Correlation  formal contract x  wage drift | 0.86 | 0.03 | -0.30 | 0.38 |
| *White-collar workers* | | | | |
| Formal contract increases | -- | -- | 6.2% | 7.3% |
| (SD) | -- | -- | (1.2) | (4.3) |
| Wage drift | -- | -- | 1.3% | 1.8% |
| (SD) | -- | -- | (0.3) | (0.8) |
| Total wage increases | -- | -- | 7.5% | 9.5% |
| (SD) | -- | -- | (1.3) | (3.8) |
| Real total wage increases | -- | -- | 2.3% | -0.7% |

Table 2.1b: System performance variables

| Variables | Epoch | | | |
|---|---|---|---|---|
| | I | II | III | IV |
| | 1946-55 | 1956-65 | 1966-73 | 1974-83 |
| *Contextual variables* | Yearly averages | | | |
| Industrial conflicts * | 174 | 18 | 185 | 536 |
| Wild-cat strikes * | -- | -- | 33 | 50 |
| Relative size LO/TCO | 4.4 | 3.4 | 2.3 | 1.8 |
| White collar degree of organization | -- | 55% | 63% | 70% |
| *Economic background variables* | | | | |
| Change in GNP | 3.8% | 4.2% | 3.4% | 1.4% |
| (SD) | (2.0) | (2.0) | (1.8) | (2.1) |
| Inflation | 4.4% | 3.7% | 5.3% | 10.3% |
| (SD) | (4.8) | (1.4) | (2.1) | (2.0) |
| Unemployment | 2.7% | 1.7% | 2.1% | 2.0% |
| (SD) | (0.4) | (0.4) | (0.4) | (0.3) |
| Change in productivity | -- | **4.8% | 4.4% | 1.4% |
| (SD) | | (1.4) | (1.1) | (1.8) |
| Change in industrial production | 5.6% | 5.7% | 4.4% | -0.2% |
| (SD) | (6.2) | (2.5) | (2.3) | (3.9) |
| Industry profits | -- | 5.7% | 4.2% | 3.2% |
| (SD) | | (0.7) | (0.8) | (2.2) |
| Public sector employment (1000's) | -- | -- | ***1057 | 1391 |
| Increase in wage taxes **** | -- | **0.8% | 1.0% | 2.3% |
| (SD) | | (0.2) | (0.6) | (2.2) |

* Working days lost in 1000s per year   ***1963-1965
**1961-1965   ****White-collar

The correlation between wage drift and agreement wages became positive in this epoch. During this period the average working days lost in industrial conflicts rose to 536 000/year from 185 000/year in the preceding epoch. A substantial part of this was due, of course, to the 'Great Conflict' of 1980. Nonetheless, other indications were the substantial increase in 'wildcat strikes' and in the number of negotiations which required mediation.

The fourth epoch is not only characterized by substantial changes in the WNS, but by a growing sense of crisis. The 1973 oil price shock and the subsequent adjustments show up strongly in the economic variables. GNP only grew by 1.4 percent on the average and productivity by 1.4 percent. Industrial production actually decreased by on the average 0.2 percent while inflation was on the average 10.3 percent. Further aggravating the picture is a deficit in government finances and sustained increases in payroll taxes (on the average 2.3 percent a year).

Our analysis of the data stresses the changes in the variance of key performance variables associated with the restructuring of the WNS in the periods we have identified. Variance was relatively low in period II, but even period III can be characterized as a period of effectively 'organized social discipline'.

One of the most striking findings is the transformation of the correlation between changes in contract wages and changes in wage drift. Wage drift, as suggested earlier, is mainly the result of local developments, within companies as a result of product market developments and comparisons in the labor market, while contract wage formation is the result of central (or in Epoch I branch) negotiations and the strategic efforts of peak organizations to steer wage developments. The correlation between wage-drift and contract wage formation was positive in the first and last periods, but zero and negative in the second and third periods, respectively.

The observed relationship in the second and third periods was the result of effectively organized control. The negative relationship in period III probably reflected the widespread use of wage development guarantees. According to these, wages and salaries were adjusted for wage-drift in the preceding year.

The positive correlation between contract wage formation and wage drift in Epoch IV indicates the inability or unwillingness of central actors to control or limit the struggle over income distribution. White-collar peak organizations as well as non-industrial blue-collar workers tried to make up in favorable central agreements for relative losses arising form wage drift which benefited industrial blue-collar workers. On the other hand, the latter attempted, through wage drift, to regain part of what private white-collar unions and public sector unions had won through formal central negotiations.

In the next chapter I will take a closer look at the developments in the last epoch and recent developments. It was during the 1980's that the employers' organizations decided to restructure the system through the return to branch level negotiations.

# 3 Wage Negotiations in Sweden: Some Recent Patterns

The nineteeneighties brought an end to the Swedish Model of wage negotiations. During this period the rule regime which had proscribed central negotiations between the peak organizations ceased to be upheld by the actors. What were the circumstances leading up to the decentralization of wage negotiations in 1983?[66] A great conflict in 1980 focused the attention to the problems which arise in a centralized negotiation system. The main problem in those negotiations was the question of the relative wage differences between different segments of the economy. A set of rules had been created starting in 1966 which made wage drift spread all over the economy through the central agreements. Instead of working as a moderator of wage increases, the central agreements became a inflatory engine. In this chapter I will analyze these different rules.

The struggle in the wage negotiation system is not only over wages. There is also a struggle over political influence. Strong central organizations which can control wage developments become interesting bargaining partners to the government. A decentralization of wage negotiations also decreases the political clout of these large organizations. What we see in this period is a struggle over the Meta-rules: What are going to be the main governing principles of the system?

## The 1980-1986 wage rounds

Up until 1983 there was a tendency to centralize wage negotiations through union cooperation within the segments. The model of central negotiations between peak organizations was taken for granted. LO used to negotiate with SAF in the private segment. PTK has since 1974 negotiated centrally for its member unions with SAF. In 1983 this pattern was changed when SIF and Metall negotiated separately with VF. In some previous negotiations LO and PTK had coordinated their negotiating efforts.

In the public segment, negotiations have been coordinated between the peak organizations since the mid-seventies. The constellation was called "the gang of four" and consisted of TCO-S, KTK, SF and SKAF. A facilitating factor has been the common wage system in the public segment, plus the existence of many common worker categories.

LO and PTK coordinated their negotiations in the wage rounds between 1977 and 1980. In 1980 the cooperation failed when LO insisted that the white-collar workers should restrain their demands and let LO-workers increase their wages further. Attempts were made in 1983 to find a compromise between the organizations but the attempts failed when the wage development guarantees were discussed.

Cooperation within the "gang of four" (the unions in the public segment) ceased as well but during a later phase of the negotiations. SF and SKAF developed a closer affinity with the other LO-unions when the wage development guarantees were discussed. This is an example of the complexity within LO. Even though LO is mainly involved in the private segment of the labor market, it has member organizations in both segments. The LO-unions operate in the private sector, in the public sector at local, county and state levels. The connections that this create can be used to push for decreasing as well as increasing the distances between the groups. The phenomena is not only confined to LO, to a lesser degree, all cartels face similar problems between its member organizations.

## The great conflict of 1980

The 1980 wage round led to one of the largest strikes ever experienced in Sweden. Despite the fact that Sweden had grown accustomed to a larger number of strikes, especially in the public segment, the size and scope of the conflict surprised many.

The central agreement between LO and SAF expired on November 1 1979. LO had started its preparations in the autumn but was not ready to present a bargaining offer. LO claimed that it was impossible to specify the wage demands due to the uncertainty about the government's economic policy. It was already early February when SAF took the initiative and sent a letter to LO where SAF proposed that the current agreements should be prolonged.[67]

The public segment unions were next to present their demands. on February 28 they demanded wage increases of at least 12%. Meanwhile LO and PTK conducted discussions about joint negotiations, which failed after PTK's large negotiation delegation could not accept that LO got substantially larger increases than PTK. LO presented a demand for 11.3% wage increases on March 7.[68]

The initiative in the 1980 negotiations was with SAF. They intended to deliver a heavy blow in the public segment . In a March 14 letter to LO, SAF responded to LO's demands by claiming that the only way to increase real wages was to reduce public expenditure. SAF wrote at the same time to the government and asked for the appointment of a special delegation to review the public expenditure.[69]

In a sauna meeting between the prime minister Fälldin and the LO and PTK chairmen, the prime minister had come to the conclusion that legislation on the wages was the only way to solve the threatened conflict. But this misunderstanding was corrected on March 26.[70]

The government intervened on March 27. They presented a six-point program which included a price-freeze, reduced taxation for low- and middle income earners and an investment fund raised from part of company profits. A precondition for the program was that the parties agreed to sign an agreement on almost unchanged terms.

Two mediating commissions had been appointed by the government: one for the private segment, and one for the public segment. These tried to coordinate their efforts and presented offers at more or less the same time.

LO had started an overtime boycott on March 27. SAF had responded with a threat of a great lock-out which was to take place from April 10 to April 16. SAF's chairman, Curt Nicolin, said to the press that the lockout was an "investment for the future". SAF agreed to postpone the lockout and the commission could start to work with a 15 öre kitty. Both LO and SAF withdrew their conflict notices.[71]

The private segment got an offer from the commission on April 23 and the public segment on April 24. LO could not accept the offer and recommended its unions to serve strike notices for a strike starting May 2. The public sector had served their notices earlier, and when TCO-S could not accept the April 24 offer, a strike erupted on April 25. The mediating commissions delivered new offers, to LO on April 29, to the public segment on April 30. While SAF accepted the offer, both LO and the public segment unions, rejected the offer.[72]

After May 2, Sweden stopped. The greatest conflict in the post-war period had begun. The mediators had presented an offer on April 29-30 which amounted to 2.3% plus a wage development guarantee. This offer was based on SAF's position. The next offer, which was finally accepted by all parties, was based on the changed position of the government. This offer amounted to 6.8% for LO. It was deemed too high by SAF, who rejected it. Only after a plea from the government did SAF agree to the terms and the conflict could end on May 11. The agreement was deemed to be too high by many observers. The unions would have settled for 1-2% less, was the conventional wisdom. The main difference between the different offers was the size of the wage development guarantee. From a small guarantee of about 1%, it grew to a guarantee of 3.5% in the final agreement.[73]

More important than the level of the agreements is the game between the segments which shaped the conflict. SAF had launched an attack on the public segment. In the March 14 letter, SAF asked for a government commission to reduce public spending. SAF especially pointed to the municipal sector as a culprit. The expanding municipalities (which have their own right to tax) were taking a larger part of income taxes. SAF also wanted to make cuts in spending on social security.[74] SAF and the government seemed to believe that the unions in the public segment could be intimidated into accepting either a low agreement or legislation over wages. When the conflict in the public segment started, the government was caught off guard. Their preparations were minimal for the conflict.[75]

SAF's strategy was, according to the municipal workers union (SKAF), to create a rift between public segment and private segment unions. Their chairman, Sigvard Marjasin wrote:

> If it was possible to stop the public sector employees now, it would be easier in the next round to take on the rest of the LO-collective. The aim was to split the coordinated wage round and to return to industry level or company level negotiations. In that way the individual company's ability to pay would alone guide the wage structure. Through playing putative group interest against each other, SAF intends, like the old imperialists, to divide and rule.

> For the same reasons, SAF was one of the most bitter opponents of the cooperation between the public sector employees.[76]

SAF's maneuvers contributed to the dead locked negotiations in the public segment according to Marjasin. Faxén, SAF's chief economist, points out that there was no abyss between LO's and SAF's estimation of the available room for increases. While SAF had accepted an offer on April 29 which would total 9%, LO had estimated the room for increases to between 10.3% and 11%. The dispute was rather about SAF's ambition to use this room to increase the competitiveness of Swedish industry.[77]

The great conflict of 1980 had its origins in the struggle between the private and public segment. The private segment maneuvered in order to force an agreement on the public segment, which would not fully compensate for the wage drift of the private segment workers. The strategy may have been to play a "chicken game" with the public segment. Through threatening a large conflict, the private segment challenged the public segment to be the ones who pushed Sweden over the brink into a large industrial conflict. The public employers' unpreparedness for the conflict is one indication of this.

SAF's strategy to contain the public segment failed. Instead they had to accept a wage agreement which was unnecessarily high. The public segment also gained an innovation, the L-ATF,[78] which together with ÅSF, created a 1% wage increase which was to be negotiated locally. In this way, the public segment got the equivalent of the private segment non-level-rising supplement (INL). The public segment achieved a 100% compensation for private sector wage developments.

The great conflict of 1980 added to the mistrust which many large companies, especially in manufacturing, felt toward the negotiation system. At the end of the 1970s, wage developments had started to get out of hand.

## The 1981 wage round

The 1981 wage round was conventional in character. SAF had already decided to decentralize bargaining in the next round to the industry level. The necessary organizational and statutory changes were not yet made. The negotiations were therefore conducted in the usual way. LO negotiated first and PTK followed suit.

For SAF, the wage round has already started in August. This is when the second quarter wage statistics are requested from their members. Already at this point SAF prepared for a return to industry level agreements.

According to an internal SAF document,[79] SAF considered the 1974 and 1978 agreements as acceptable, while the 1975 and 1980 agreements were considered disastrous. SAF's starting point in negotiations is that the agreements have to reflect the realities of the economy. In this sense, the 1980 agreement allowed the control to slip away from the labor market actors. SAF felt itself cornered by the public segment. The only alternative to negotiations was a government incomes policy.

SAF experienced the white-collar workers as a new powerful group. This group could obstruct production through taking a small group of vital employees out on strike. The complicated system of wage development guarantees made the system inflexible. SAF experienced that the unions were able to implement their own wage policy to a large degree.

Already in August 1980 there were plans to change the system in order to get away from the blockages they felt were hindering it. The strategy was to return to industry level negotiations for a couple of wage rounds, thereby shaking the system and making it more flexible.

The EFO-model[80] had been a guideline for wage negotiations in Sweden but SAF was accused of deviating from this in 1980. SAF had aimed at improving the profit situation of industry. One of the preconditions of the EFO-model was that there was an agreement on the proper size of the profit share compared to the wage share of the surplus of production. Now that SAF wanted to improve the profit share the EFO model was, according to SAF, no longer applicable. The EFO-model was however of great importance to the public segment. It allowed them to independently assess the room for wage increases and thus allowed them some initiative in the wage rounds. Björn Rosengren, the chairman of KTK found it necessary to defend the EFO-model in October.

In November SAF discussed the preconditions for the 1981 wage round. SAF estimated the effects of previous agreements and wage drift for this year to amount to 7% which would leave 2% to be negotiated about, on condition that wage and price developments in competing countries were above 9%. SAF thought that these 2% together with a three-year agreement, would raise profitability to an acceptable level, that is, if the companies were to distribute the remaining 2%.

LO's general council[81] decided on a bargaining package on November 18. They assumed that the economy would grow 2% in 1981. The change in tax-rates which the government was preparing, international developments forced LO to demand high monetary wages in order to protect the interests of low-paid workers. LO estimated the cost of the agreement at 10%.[82]

The unions in the public segment and PTK presented their proposals late November - early December. PTK wanted to find out if its member unions were allowed to strike after SAF and PTK had signed an agreement.

LO formally asked for negotiations with SAF on December 15. SAF and LO were well ahead of both PTK and the public segment in this wage round. SAF was interested in a three-year agreement, while LO was not so keen on the idea. The differences between the parties had to do with the length of the agreement, the negotiation procedure and the level of the agreement. The parties anticipated a devaluation during 1981 and worked

on a design for a price guarantee. It was not until January 15 1981, that
SAF could formally announce that SAF wanted to negotiate centrally with
LO.[83]

The negotiations proceeded smoothly and on February 2 the agreement was signed. The agreement was estimated to give wage increases of
3.6% in 1981 and 3.5% in 1982.

During the LO-SAF negotiations, nothing happened on the PTK-front.
PTK had wanted to postpone negotiations and the question of its
members' right to strike after an agreement was signed, proved to be a
suitable instrument to delay the actual negotiations. PTK's large negotiating delegation approved a solution to the question on February 20. PTK
was ready to present a bid to the employers on March 2.[84]

SAF and PTK negotiated in March and SAF could deliver an offer to
PTK on the 26th. The proposal included a price guarantee and a wage
guarantee similar to those in the agreement between SAF and LO.[85] PTK
did not accept the offer and the negotiations broke down. A mediating
commission was appointed by the government. The mediating commission
presented a final bid on the 21st, which PTK dismissed. The main problem
seems to have been the form of the wage development guarantee. PTK got
a second final offer on May 2 and a third final offer on the 10th. The
important difference here was the design of the wage development
guarantee. PTK managed to get a clause linking its wages to LO's wage
development.[86]

PTK accepted the offer on May 11. Before the ink on the agreement
had dried, SAF was busy discussing the form of the coming wage round.
The 1981 wage round had been fairly conventional. LO started out,
followed later by PTK. But SAF had already at this stage decided to go
along with VF's initiative to decentralize negotiations. The necessary
statutory changes had not been made, but the preparations were in an
advanced state.

## The 1983 wage round: Partial Decentralization

SAF changed its statutes in June 1982 at an extra congress: SAF could no
longer demand to ratify agreements negotiated by member employers'
associations. The employers' associations were also given the right to
declare lock-outs.

The change in statutes may be mostly of a symbolic character. Clause
32 in SAF's statutes still gives some authority to SAF. The clause gives
SAF the right to give instructions regarding the contents of collective

agreements and general procedures. The contradiction in the statutes can be interpreted as an attempt by SAF to reserve to itself the right to the final determination of the content of agreements and the negotiation procedure at the same time as the member associations are given the freedom to negotiate separately within the boundaries of SAF policy.[87] VF is the organization which had the initiative and pushed for the change. There does not seem to be any great disagreement within SAF about the change.

The change of statutes allowed SAF to deviate from the negotiation procedures which had remained in power since 1956. The employers were ready to try industrial level negotiations.

LO had contacted the white-collar workers' cartels to discuss government tax and social security policies. The wage development guarantees were also on the agenda. PTK had problems with SALF, the foremen's union. SALF decided to leave PTK and to form a separate central organization. In the autumn elections of 1982, a social democratic government was elected. LO presented their wage demands on November 25 at the meeting of LO's general council. A formal offer was presented to SAF on December 15. But SAF gave no response other than a request to meet the government to discuss economic policy. LO and PTK did not want to join such a meeting.[88]

In January 1983 an impartial committee arrived at a judgment of the PTK - SALF conflict. They were of the opinion that SALF acted contrary to the statutes of PTK by seeking to create their own central organization. Shortly thereafter the labor court decided against PTK's interpretation of the wage development guarantee.[89]

SAF delivered a zero-level proposal on January 20, but said they were willing to negotiate about compensation for temporary dismissal, provisions for persons who were forced to change job tasks and jobs for young persons. LO rejected SAF's offer and SAF established that they can not participate in central negotiations. PTK awaited developments before giving any response.[90]

SAF's refusal to negotiate centrally and VF's initiative to negotiate on the industrial level, ended 27 years of repeated central negotiations between LO and SAF. In February VF and Metall started to negotiate. Metall tried to show solidarity with the LO collective and opened with the same proposal as LO had tried earlier.

VF did not immediately offer a wage increase. VF started instead to offer Metall a number of changes in the industrial level agreement, a number of issues for which Metall had struggled for years.

Meanwhile LO tried to coordinate the wage round through its industrial unions. LO discerned that the different unions were offered proposals of varying size and form. To move ahead, LO announced a February 16 deadline. At the meeting of the general council and the executive board on the 16th, all industrial level negotiations, with the exception of Metall, were declared to have broken down. SAF's large negotiation delegation wanted SAF and LO to form a mediating commission. LO rejected the initiative and announced strike notices for nine unions.[91]

SAF still wanted negotiations to take place at the industry level, and thereafter, mediation at the industrial level, but LO was not in a position to yield. In this situation, the government appointed a mediating commission for those LO-SAF areas where negotiations had broken down. The mediating commission was able to present a bid already on March 2. LO wanted to discuss the bid while SAF rejected it.[92]

VF wanted to negotiate no matter what it would take. VF delivered substantial offers and proposed to solve a lot of long overdue problems. It would have been difficult for Metall to go on strike for the principle of centralized negotiations. Many of the advances in the negotiations would have been jeopardized if negotiations were to break down. It was clearly of value for Metall to sign an agreement separately with VF.

The VF-Metall agreement was signed on March 5. Metall got more beneficial terms for workers eligibility for holiday wages. Earlier workers had to work both before and after the holiday in order to get paid during the holiday. This was a question which Metall had struggled over since 1955. The Metall-VF agreement also devised a fourth wage group, and shortened working hours for shift workers. VF got the option to vary working hours across the year.[93]

There was no wage drift guarantee in the agreement. VF took a staunch position against such guarantees. These guarantees did not, however, usually give much to Metall workers. It was beneficial both to VF and Metall to negotiate separately in 1983. The reactions from other unions were mixed. The agreement did not differ much from the rest LO-SAF agreement. The low-wage unions were however concerned about the future if there were not to be any low-wage supplements.[94]

Already on March 9 both LO and SAF accepted the bid offered by the mediating commission, SAF did not, however, want the wage development guarantee. Persuaded by the government, SAF yielded on the evening of March 11.[95]

The public segment could sign an agreement on March 18. Meanwhile the white-collar workers had moved ahead in their negotiations. As on the blue-collar workers' side, VF had the initiative and negotiated separately with SIF, SALF and CF.[96]

At the end of March and beginning of April, VF initiated negotiations with the white-collar workers. LO, Metall, and the public segment had already signed agreements. PTK's general council had established in February that SAF did not have any mandate to negotiate, and that the offers LO had received were too low. Instead of risking being forced into a mediation, PTK choose not to negotiate. Instead they started an information campaign about the white-collar workers' poor wage development in real terms. In discussions with SAF, PTK received acknowledgement for their real wage development and announced that they wanted to disconnect themselves from LO's wage development. This was to be achieved through a long-term agreement.[97]

On April 13 SAF was able to invite PTK to negotiations, in which SAF represented all except VF and the ship-owners. VF had already started negotiations with SIF and CF on March 14. VF presented an offer on March 31. SIF's large negotiation delegation discussed the offer on April 7. They considered the offer to be too low. Instead of countering with an offer of their own, SIF awaited developments in the SAF-PTK negotiations.[98]

It was not until June 6 that an agreement could be signed between SAF and PTK. There were a couple of novelties in the agreement. It was divided into two periods of 17 and 12 months length. The white-collar workers were divided into two groups. Those who earned more than 10800 Kronor a month were excluded from the agreement. This caused considerable problems when SIF's general council was to ratify the agreement. The division of SIF into two groups was seen as a threat against centralized negotiations and as a threat to the coherence of the organization. SIF had been struggling for a reduction of wage differentials within the union. This 'solidaristic' wage policy was now threatened. Employees with low wages were given too little, and the agreement should be in Kronor instead of percentages, according to the critics. Eventually SIF ratified the agreement by a slim margin.[99]

The negotiations with VF were not finished. SIF could now use the SAF-PTK agreement as a base to stand on. One week after the ratification of the SAF-PTK agreement, SIF was ready to sign an agreement with VF.

## The 1984 wage round

Elvander (1988) claims that after the return to industry level negotiations in the 1983 wage round, it became less and less self-evident that wage negotiations should be centralized. In the 1984 wage round, LO tried to coordinate the industry level negotiations of its member unions. The government tried to stabilize the WNS acting through the employers in the public sector. In the middle of March 1984, two-year agreements were signed for the public sector employees. The level of the agreements were high due to the mutual distrust and monitoring between the public and private sector actors.[100]

The prologue to the 1984 wage agreements start with the adjustment of the tax-rates which the government initiated in November 1983. Taxes were raised for those earning more than 125.000 Kronor a year. In this way, the government appeased LO while intimidating white-collar workers and the political parties (liberals and the center-party) with whom the government had earlier reached a common understanding on the tax issue.[101] As a consequence of the tax change, LO's demands could be lowered to about 7% instead of the original 11%. PTK was also inclined to lower their aspirations and was ready to settle for an agreement that would make the government goal of a 4% inflation ceiling for 1984 possible .[102]

The first negotiations were those between the parties in the public segment. The government tried to introduce a two-year agreement which would assist the goal of a 4% inflation ceiling 1984 and 3% for 1985.

The public segment agreements were signed in March 1984. The unions had managed to remove the limit on the wage drift guarantee and the 1% deduction for structural changes when calculating the basis for the guarantee. They also managed to get a re-negotiation clause which would be enacted if the private segment blue-collar workers agreements were to result in a higher level than their own.[103]

The losers in the 1984 agreement in the public segment were the white-collar workers within SACO/SR. The higher paid university graduates got a relatively poor agreement due to the concentration on low paid workers in the agreement.[104]

At the same time, Metall was negotiating with VF. Metall aimed at a one year agreement so as not to get out of step with the white-collar workers in SIF, SALF and CF whose agreement ended in May 1984. The Metall chairman wanted an agreement which was not less than what had been obtained in the public segment. The ceiling thus became the floor for the following negotiations. An agreement was signed on March 21.[105]

Figure 3.1:  Agreement Lengths 1984-1985

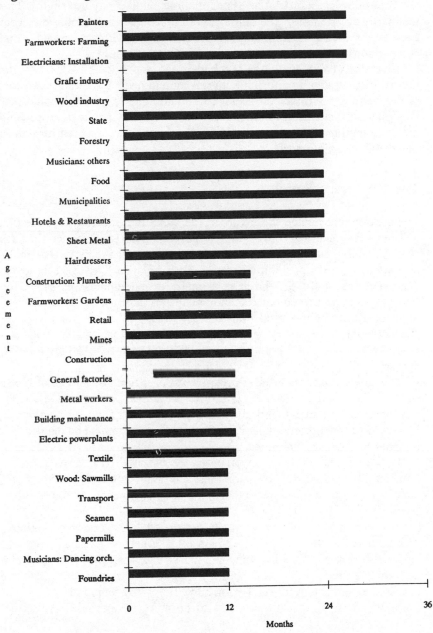

The following industrial level negotiations all had varying lengths. This was partly an attempt by the employers to de-couple the negotiations from each other. With varying lengths of agreements, it was thought that comparisons could not be made so easily. (See figure 3.1)

Elvander (1988) attributes the high wage agreements of 1984 to the mutual distrust and monitoring between the unions in the different sectors of the economy. Without the usual coordination by LO, Metall could play its opponents against the public sector, while the public sector could motivate high increases through comparisons with the expected turnout in the Metall negotiations.[106]

## The 1985 wage round

The government invited the actors in the WNS to a meeting on June 6th, Sweden's National day. This symbolic day was used to introduce the idea of a 5% ceiling on wage increases for 1985. At a later meeting on June 26, all parties agreed upon the 5% limit. Both LO and SAF were ready to negotiate, taking the 5% limit as a goal. An agreement was signed on February 8. The agreement recommended the industrial unions to negotiate for 1985 within a total limit of 5%. Industrial peace was no longer guaranteed for the following negotiations. In contrast to the 1956-1981 central agreements, the unions now had the right to strike if they found it necessary.[107]

The government imposed a prize freeze on March 6. The idea was to restrain Metall from including a price development guarantee in the agreement being negotiated. It was possible to sign an agreement on March 18 between Metall and VF after Metall had dropped its demand for a price development guarantee.[108]

In the subsequent local negotiations the 5% limit was surpassed. The limit had pushed down wage increases, but could not, in the view of VF, control local wage developments. There the 5% limit became a starting-point.[109]

VF had in the 1983 wage round succeeded in negotiating separately with SIF, SALF and CF (all members of PTK). PTK had negotiated an agreement with SAF for its other members. The agreement was to expire on May 31 1985. SIF, SALF and CF negotiated with VF in 1984 and reached an agreement for the period July 7 1984 - December 31 1985. PTK wanted a short agreement in order to be able to harmonize the agreements with the other unions. On May 29 1985 PTK and SAF signed a preliminary agreement which one month later was ratified.[110]

The public segment employees had reached an agreement with the employers which had a re-negotiation clause: "Ventilen". It stated that negotiations were to be re-opened if the LO-SAF agreement for manufacturing industry were to exceed their own agreement. This crude wage development guarantee was to cause a large conflict which erupted on May 2. TCO-S was the only organization which went on strike. The strike lasted until May 20. TCO-S achieved what it intended: its wages were to follow the development of wages for private employees. TCO-S got a 2% compensation compared to its 3.1% claim. TCO-S had been on its own, this was a breakdown of cooperation between the unions in the public segment.[111]

The public segment agreements meant that the 5% limit was largely exceeded. The public segment employees got raises of up to 10% for this, the second year of the agreement. This was compared to 1984, when the private employees got a much more favorable development.[112]

## The 1986 wage round

The 1986 negotiations were to be conducted separately for the private and the public segment. PTK and LO coordinated their negotiations for the first time since 1978. PTK and SAF signed an agreement on April 10, while LO and SAF signed an agreement on April 11. Both agreements were for two years ahead. Metall had more difficulties in negotiating with VF. An agreement was signed until June 6 under impending threats of strikes and lockouts.[113]

The public segment negotiations were opened thereafter but were not as successful. A strike by SACO/SR broke out on May 22 which was met by the employers with a threat of a large lock-out of teachers. The conflict was postponed during the summer. A larger strike erupted in the autumn with TCO-S SF KTK and SKAF. One of the stumbling blocks was the question of compensation for private sector wage developments. The government managed to evade a wage development guarantee of the kind which had been used earlier. If wages in the public sector were lagging behind, they would have to be corrected in the following wage round. The public sector employees got two other advantages as well: they managed to raise the salaries of top level employees, and managed to decentralize the negotiation system to some degree.[114]

# Linking the negotiations together

There are many rules used in central agreements which links the negotiations and the agreements to each other. There has been a tendency during the seventies to elaborate these rules and introduce them in new areas. In a way these rules are used to control insecurity. Central agreements nevertheless, there is a free-zone where wages or their buying power can change irrespective of the central agreement. The most common connection has been the different wage development guarantees. These were introduced in the 1966 LO-SAF agreement and have since then developed and spread all over the labor market, as will be described in a later section.

The agreements can also be made contingent on government policy, as is the intention behind price development guarantees. These serve two purposes: first, they can act as a shield against inflation, but secondly, they can be an incentive for the government to combat inflation. In this way they can be a stabilizing force. When they are triggered by unforeseen price developments, they may further destabilize the economy.

The rule regime which made these guarantees necessary was the one which aimed to centralize wage negotiations. In decentralized negotiations, each group can argue for compensation without making reference to such rules.

Another set of rules which links negotiations together is found in the institution of mediation committees. In 1980 he LO-SAF negotiations were connected through mediation committees to the public segment negotiations. There are specific rules which controls the way these committees are brought into the negotiations. In order for a mediation committee to be called in to a negotiation, negotiation must have started and the parties must have asked the government to name a committee. It is a way to get further in negotiations, avoiding costly conflicts, but it has also created an opportunity to draw unwilling organizations into attempts at larger coordination efforts. In order not to be forced into a negotiation committee, the organization must wait to start their negotiations.

The order in which the negotiations take place is important. There is always the possibility that unions in later negotiations get better agreements. The organizations have attempted to control this factor of insecurity through clauses in the agreement that allows for re-negotiations if other organizations get different terms or if the preconditions for the negotiations change too much. The different unions compete for their share of wage increases. Their wage policies differ, and so do their members' opinions, which will be discussed in more detail in chapter five.

The rivalry between the unions is evident in the various wage development guarantees, which will be presented in the next section.

## Connecting agreements and economic policy: price development guarantees

The unions may try to protect themselves with various price indexation clauses in their agreements. The central wage negotiations were partly developed because of price indexation practices. The post World War I inflation led to the introduction of bonus supplements to compensate workers for the rising cost of living. These supplements increased to the extent that a large part of the wage was made independent of the work effort. In 1917 percentage increases in wage agreements were introduced. During the second World War, LO demanded that wages should be protected against decreases in real terms. As a result, price guarantees were introduced in the agreements. These guarantees were used up until 1952. There was also a price guarantee in the 1957 agreement. These guarantees were absent from Swedish wage negotiations until 1977 when they were reintroduced. There were price development guarantee in all SAF-LO agreements up to 1983.[115]

The different rules in the form of price development guarantees serve a double purpose: first they are a guarantee that wage earners get compensated for price increases, but secondly, they are an incentive for the government to pursue a policy which moderates price developments. Price development guarantees constrain the government's pursuit of political and economical policies which affect the price level. It becomes more dangerous to raise indirect taxes, to devalue, and to increase prices for public utilities. Price guarantees may thus operate as an instrument to stabilize the government's economic policy. This is especially important in a situation where the government and the labor market organizations have little confidence in each other. The economic policy of the government in the period 1976-1982 showed a great deal of unpredictability. In fact, the government changed the preconditions for the agreements after they were signed. In such a situation price guarantees may act as a form of insurance.

Price development guarantees may also destabilize the economy. When they fail to help to control price developments, i.e. when they are applied, they lead to wage increases which will further amplify the inflationary process.

## Connecting agreements and wage drift: wage development guarantees

In the central agreements before 1966 there were no formal wage development guarantees. Wage drift was during this period a large part of the total wage development. VF proposed in 1963 that the agreements should determine the gross wage increases, that is, wage drift was to be subtracted from the agreed wage increases when applying central agreements. In the 1964 wage round this initiative was not seriously considered due to, among other things, the restrictive pose taken by the employers.[116]

Wage development guarantees were placed on the agenda of central negotiations between SAF and LO in 1966 for the first time. Eight different SAF-constructions were discussed and a number of constructions from the mediating committee. A model was chosen where wage drift was not deducted from regular increases. The consequence was instead that wage drift was incorporated in the central agreements![117]

From 1966 until 1982 wage development guarantees were regularly used in the central agreements. The background to the introduction of these guarantees was the increasing stream of exceptions from central agreements before 1966. When some industries and categories of workers had experienced a slower development of wages than others, these problems had to be solved ahead of central negotiations. It was difficult to compensate these groups in the industry level negotiations, since the level of raises was fixed and the parties did not have the right to take up industrial action. The exceptions tended to increase and to involve more detailed negotiations. The advent of wage development guarantees made negotiations more effective.[118]

Rules are introduced in order to control or guide some phenomena. The introduction of wage development guarantee rules reflect the central actors lack of control over wage developments. During the 1970s, central agreements between LO and SAF were only responsible for slightly more than half of blue-collar workers total wage increases.

The wage development guarantees are themselves a vehicle of wage drift. If a company restricts wage drift, they will have to increase wages later due to the wage development guarantees. It can be tempting to allow wage drift so as to anticipate the wage development guarantee.

Wage development guarantees for white-collar workers and for employees in the public sector have included blue-collar workers wage development guarantees as a target. The connections between the agreements led to a situation where disturbances such as wage drift were rather rapidly distributed all over the system.

## The SAF-LO Wage development guarantees

The first wage development guarantee[119] was introduced in the 1966 collective agreement between LO and SAF. It was applied in the following year. It was calculated on the wage drift for the manufacturing industry,[120] no difference was made between time-wages, piece-wages, holiday wages, and shift work wages.[121]

The first year of the agreement did not have a wage development guarantee. The guarantee applied to the second year of the agreement, and was based on the statistics for the first year. The regular agreement for the first year included considerations for wage drift compensation. The wage development guarantee was to be calculated for each area which was covered by an industry level agreement.[122]

In 1969 the base for calculation was changed from the area which was covered by an industry level agreement to each company. The supplemental wages paid for shift work were excluded from the calculations.[123]

In 1974 the wage development guarantee was changed so that it was to be applied after the year which was covered by the regular central agreement. This phenomena was to be called an "overhang". Each following central agreement had to take into consideration the wage development guarantee of the preceding agreement. [124]

In the 1975 agreement the guarantee was changed so that the base for calculation was time-wages and piece-wages separately at each company. Up until this agreement the wage development guarantees had been constructed on the basis of a reference level. If wage drift did not exceed this level, wages should be raised with the difference between their own wage drift and this level. The actual wage drift was not known at the time when these levels were fixed. The outcome of these guarantees therefore differed from year to year.[125]

In 1978 the method of calculation was changed. Instead of a reference level, compensation based on a fixed percentage of actual wage drift was used as a target for the guarantee. The figure of 80% of the actual wage drift was agreed upon. As a consequence, the degree of compensation for others' wage drift rose from 60% to 80%. In the 1980 agreement holiday wages were removed from the calculation of the wage development guarantee. The different number of holidays from year to year had caused a fluctuation in the calculations. In the 1981 agreement, the calculation method was changed back to a reference level.[126]

Figure 3.2:   The Structure of Wage Development Guarantees

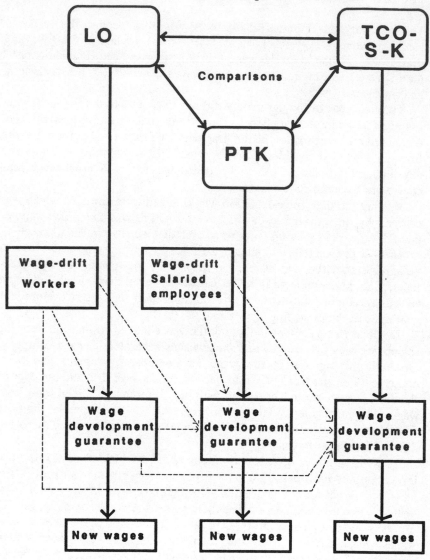

## The wage development guarantees of the white-collar workers

Wage development guarantees serve another purpose for the white-collar unions. For them, the purpose of the guarantees is also to guard their relative wage level compared to blue-collar workers. In the five year agreement between ISAM and SAF, there was a clause which allowed for adjustments of wages if the blue-collar workers' wage development had exceeded the development for white-collar workers by more than 1% in the period 1971-1972. Wages for 1973 and 1974 were subsequently changed.[127]

The wage development guarantee was in 1975 applied at the company level. The wages were compared to blue-collar workers' wages at the company. In the regular agreement there was a provision for 4.1% of increases due to blue-collar workers' wage drift. This had to be deducted in the calculation of the guarantee. Only if blue-collar workers' wage drift exceeded white-collar workers' wage drift plus 4.1% was the agreement to be applied.[128]

In the wage development guarantee for 1976 wages were to be compared within the group of white-collar workers. This guaranteed that wages were to be raised with 3.2%. Part from this, white-collar workers were to be compensated if blue-collar workers in their company drifted more than 2.8% and if their relative wage level was disadvantageous. The wage development guarantee for 1977 became a controversy in the negotiations between SAF and PTK. PTK wanted 100% compensation for worker's wage drift. Eventually a compensation of 80% was agreed upon. PTK members were to be given a compensation which was 80% of the sum of: blue-collar workers' wage drift, the blue-collar workers' wage development guarantee and industry level agreements above the central agreement. The construction of 1978 and 1979 remained the same as the 1977 construction.[129]

In 1980 a kitty of 1.2% was introduced. This was to be a payment in advance to compensate for blue-collar workers' wage drift. There was also a clause in the agreement which said that the developments in other negotiations (SAF-LO) was to be studied in the year to come. In 1981 the mediating commission created a retroactive guarantee for 1980, which was coupled to the wages of white-collar workers, not blue-collar workers' wages. If wage drift during 1980 did not rise more than 1.6%, wages should be raised to this level.

Figure 3.3:   Wage Development Guarantees 1966-1982

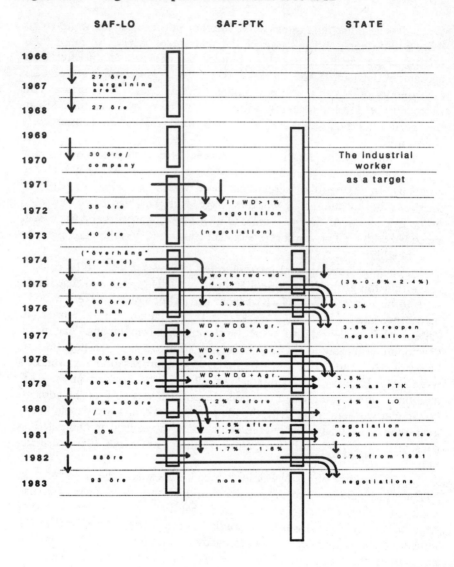

The agreement had further a guarantee for 1981 which amounted to 1.7%. In 1982 a guarantee was developed which amounted to 1.7%. There was also a clause which stated that if blue-collar workers' wage drift exceeded 8%, an extra guarantee of 1.6% should be applied.[130]

## Guarantees within the public segment.

Before wage development guarantees were introduced in the public segment, the unions pursued a policy which aimed at linking their wage development to that of blue-collar workers. From 1971 there were clauses in the agreement between the state and the unions which permitted re-negotiation of the agreement if the development of wages in the labor market as a whole, deviated considerably from the preconditions in the agreement. In 1974 this clause was applied for the first time. At that time there was a clause which used a level of 3% from which 0.6% was deducted for other adjustments.[131]

In the agreement for 1975-1976, there was a clause which led to new negotiations and amounted to 3.3% increases in 1976. The agreement of also led to a 3.6% increase in 1977. The wage development in 1977 did not lead to the use of any guarantee. In the 1978-1979 agreement there was a clause which uses the reference level from PTK without deduction of the wage drift within PTK. In 1980 the agreement employed LO's reference level with a deduction of 60 öre.

In 1981-1982 there was a clause in the agreement which called for new negotiations if the wage development in the SAF-LO and SAF-PTK areas significantly exceeded the public segment wage development. These clauses led to raises of 0.9% in 1981 and 0.7% in 1982.[132]

At first the wage development guarantee was a technique used only internally in the LO-SAF negotiations. Later, PTK elaborated a guarantee that compensated for blue-collar workers' wage drift, their guarantees and for wage drift for PTK's unions as well. In the public segment similar guarantees were developed. The effect was to systematize and lock the relative wage structure between the organizations. It was difficult for the LO collective to raise their wages more than other groups. The guarantees were one symptom of the changed nature of the system. Instead of a struggle between labor and capital over the distribution of the surplus between profits and wages, the struggle became one between the different unions in the different segments of the economy.

## Institutional innovation, metagames, and legitimacy

One important factor behind the restructuring of the Swedish wage negotiation system has been the increasing influence of public sector
employees. White-collar workers in the public segment did not receive the
right to strike and to negotiate until 1966. Earlier they had by and large
followed SAF-LO agreements. Now they have established themselves as
powerful actors in the wage negotiation system. The development of the
"gang of four"[133] was made possible. The public segment directly links
wage negotiations to the political process. Low increase in public segment
productivity creates a strain on public finances and therefore influence
taxes and inflation. The public segment is easier for the government to
influence, as the government is one of the largest employers, but at the
same time, the government becomes an easy victim for different forms of
"blackmail". A government must consider its prospects for re-election and
cannot act too harshly against half of the population: those working in the
public segment.

The character of central negotiations changed, as we have shown
earlier, in the 1970s. The white-collar workers employed by state and local
authorities got the right to strike In 1966, which they immediately used in
order to negotiate high increases for some categories such as teachers. The
expansion of the public sector further fueled the growth of the white-collar
workers' organizations. TCO more than doubled its membership between
1969 and 1980. Simultaneously the LO organization for the employees of
local authorities (SKAF) expanded and developed into LO's largest
member union

As the white-collar workers' unions grew, LO's relative size decreased
from 78% of all organized employees in 1960 to 64% in 1980. LO can no
longer dominate the wage rounds. There are new actors who, to a large
extent, can influence developments. The cartels of white-collar workers,
KTK, TCO-S, and PTK, gained in influence. From a situation where LO
together with SAF could to a great degree influence the agreements over
the whole labor market, a new situation sprung up where the wage round
turned into an equation which would have to be solved between private
and public sector LO unions, white-collar workers in the public sector,
white-collar workers in the private sector and employers in all sectors.

Table 3.1:   Development of union membership.

| Organization | 1950 | 1960 | 1970 | 1980 |
|---|---|---|---|---|
| LO | 1,278,409 | 1,485,738 | 1,680,135 | 2,126,793 |
| (Metall) | 220,114 | 270,026 | 370,146 | 454,543 |
| (SKAF) | 85,949 | 119,058 | 231,247 | 514,515 |
| SAC | 19,870 | 17,607 | 23,482 | 18,221 |
| SACO/SR | | | | 224,825 |
| TCO | 271,802 | 393,526 | 657,725 | 958,964 |
| (SIF) | 59,681 | 107,136 | 205,951 | 276,688 |
| (SKTF) | 21,047 | 31,512 | 64,238 | 146,128 |
| (ST) | | | 66,578 | 117,343 |
| Total | 1,570,081 | 1,896,871 | 2,361,342 | 3,328,803 |

Source: Micheletti (1983)

The wage structure and the wage distribution differ between the various unions. The proportion of low-paid workers is larger in municipalities than in state authorities. An endeavor to raise the wages of those with the lowest pay will be cheap for state authorities while it will be costly for municipalities and regional authorities. The wage span within PTK is large. PTK negotiates for top managers as well as for office clerks. When PTK increases wages for its low wage groups, skilled workers may feel that they are falling behind.

The Swedish model for wage negotiations presupposed a growth economy. Economic growth could reconcile demands for a reasonable return on capital, increased real wages and a growing public sector. At the same time, the system of wage negotiations contributed to economic growth. The tranquil labor market and the structural effects of the solidaristic wage policy eased economic growth.

When economic growth slowed down, the equation got more difficult to solve. Increasing demands from the public sector put a squeeze on wage developments. If wages were to rise enough to accomplish gains in real terms, this would decrease the competitiveness of Swedish industry. If industry were to keep its competitiveness, real wages would have to decline.

A situation developed where none of the parties in the negotiation process could reach their goals. When the room for real wage increases diminishes, comparisons between organizations become more important. The negotiations become a zero-sum game. It is rational for all union organizations to demand higher increases than the other organizations. The end result is however irrational: the result is only an inflationary process. A situation evolved which in game-theory is called a prisoner's dilemma game.

This setting encouraged initiatives from the employers. Dissatisfaction was growing within SAF. Employers were angered that SAF had allowed the "cost-explosion" of 1974-1976 to occur. In 1976 the chairman, Tryggve Holm, was replaced with the industrialist Curt Nicolin. This was the token of a tougher climate which eventually culminated in the great conflict of 1980. This conflict was a failure for SAF. SAF had tried to force through an agreement which would have reduced the linkages between the wage developments of the private and public segment, but it ended in a major and costly conflict and an agreement which from SAF's horizon was both expensive and mediocre.[134]

Within VF, the large exporting companies, including Volvo, started to wonder whether central negotiations were the right form for wage determination. A process was started which led to the resumption of industry level negotiations. One of the ideas was to de-couple the wage development between different industries. When wage developments were adapted to company and industry conditions, they could be contained within economically sound limits.

## The Present Crisis and the Uncertain Future

Institutions, even the most successful ones must change, because the world around them changes. They also change because the social actors engaged in them, and their power relationships, change. The actors learn and develop new goals and strategies and, as a result, place new demands on the institutions. In this context, it is essential to see institutions as human devices, social rule systems, which enable diverse actors - even agents with somewhat different perspectives and interests - to coordinate their decisions and actions, to solve common problems and to resolve social conflicts in relatively effective ways.

The Swedish collective bargaining system was designed to reduce and regulate conflicts between employers' and employees' organizations. It was never designed to deal - and the experience of the past 20 years has shown it incapable of dealing - with serious conflicts between labor groups and organizations, in particular between white-collar and blue-collar unions, as well as between collectives in the private sector as opposed to those in the public sector. As a whole, the system is segmented, with disorganized or uncoordinated but inter-linked, indirect negotiations. This has contributed to the 'wage carousel', with leapfrogging and instability as various labor unions and collectives struggle to stay ahead of or to catch up with one another.

The current complex of problems are institutional in character. One may speak of a mismatch between the institutional set-up and the typical problems and conflicts to be handled. Such mismatches give rise to innovations and attempts to restructure the set-up. Often, such restructuring leads to serious group conflicts, in part about the types of innovation required to shape a genuinely new and effective system. At the present time in Sweden there is a stalemate around the maintenance/transformation of the system. On the one hand, the established Swedish model is unable to deal effectively with a set of new and difficult problems. On the other, key actors such as the state, VF, LO, SAF, etc. are unable either to impose their respective proposals for solution or to agree to common organizing principles which could serve as a legitimizing point of departure for the establishment of a new system. In part, this is because of the absence of a dominant actor or coalition to establish and develop a new system, with new understandings and new principles and rules. The key actors and groups on the scene (e.g. the VF, major export companies, Metall, LO, white-collar unions on the private side, those on the public side, and the state) have very different ideas or confused ideas about how a new system should be organized, for instance, to what extent it should be centralized (and, in a certain sense, a continuation of the present system); or what relationships should obtain between the private and public segments; and what principles - or more precisely, what ranking of principles - of distributive justice should prevail in income determination (see Table 5.6 and 5.7)

In my view, then, one of the major shortcomings, if not the major one, of the Swedish Model is its inability to regulate or resolve destabilizing conflicts among labor unions and struggles between public and private segments over income distribution.

The segmented collective bargaining system with powerful independent unions making relative comparisons and struggling with one another - often indirectly through negotiations with employers - generates a difficult and in a certain sense unpredictable, wage negotiation process. From the perspective of many employers and employees in the export and open sectors of the economy, the system is ineffective and, indeed, entails considerable risks. If the outcomes of wage negotiation games are not predictable, a realistic planning of labor cost developments and investment decisions is no longer feasible. Thus, one important motivation sustaining the system weakens or disappears, thereby eroding commitment to the system among some major actors. Moreover, there are powerful tendencies in the system to generate wage agreements which ignore some of the pressing demands and constraints of international markets and export branches.

Major export companies such as Volvo, Electrolux, Eriksson, among others, as well as the export sector as a whole are interested in establishing a wage negotiation system - and rules of the game - which stress increased productivity, flexibility in dealing with market and competitive demands, and reliability (as a basis for long-term planning).

In this context, VF's moves to decentralize collective bargaining, to branch and possibly enterprise level, at least in VF's area, are understandable. Some labor groups and unions have supported this initiative tacitly or found it sufficiently attractive - in terms of favorable wage structure and employment conditions - to go along with the effort (e.g. Metall and SIF). Nonetheless, VF's meta-power to restructure the collective bargaining system - or to 'pull out' to a certain extent - is very circumscribed, particularly since they will sooner or later be forced to deal with the government and public sector unions who have a rather different vision of what should be done. (Of course, a strong, conservative government with a mandate to intervene in wage negotiations would be in a position to facilitate VF's efforts, but this does not appear politically likely in the foreseeable future.) While there is general dissatisfaction with the collective bargaining system, a clear, potentially stable alternative has yet to be formulated let alone find general support.

The questions facing Sweden today concern: the ways in which wage negotiations should be organized over the entire labor market, what basic principles or policies are to govern 'wage demands' and 'relative income developments' in the system, and what are appropriate levels of wage demand and development under various economic contingencies. Different agents or groups push and shove for substantially different systems: more or less decentralization, more initiative in the private sector as opposed to more in the public, greater versus less income differentials, and so forth.

Many of the conflicts in the Swedish WNS deals with the relative wage developments between different organizations. The deviance from the agreements: 'wage drift' is one of the main reasons behind the obsession with comparisons between different unions. Uncontrolled wage drift easily disturbs the existing wage differentials and may counteract the aims of the unions. The wage drift phenomena is discussed in more detail in the next chapter.

# 4 Deviance From Central Norms: Wage Drift

## Background and Definition of Wage Drift

One of the destabilizing factors in the Swedish wage negotiation system is the wage drift phenomena. Central wage agreements are negotiated norms which however do not fully govern the development of wages. It is possible to calculate the difference between what the agreement stipulates and actual wage developments. In most cases wages are found to have increased more than was agreed. Wages are said to have drifted upward. This difference is usually called "wage drift".

Wage drift is officially defined as the difference between the actual development of wages as measured between two given periods and the estimated implications of wage agreements between unions and employers at central or industry levels.[135]

Wage drift has been of major concern in the centralized wage negotiation system. Before 1966, SAF and LO negotiated exceptions from the central agreement in advance of the regular negotiations. The small negotiation committees would discuss the wage development for groups which had not had wage drift on a level comparable to other groups. The unions within LO announced in advance that they wanted to make exceptions for certain groups. After a while these negotiations expanded and the central negotiators became preoccupied with solving minuscule problems which really belonged to quite a different level. Eventually the "wage development guarantee" technique was developed.[136]

Wage drift is a free-zone and as such offers a possibility for smaller groups within the collectives to push ahead. Under piece-wages, the individual blue-collar workers have the power to decide their own wages to a higher degree than under time-wages.

The local unions have reasons not to oppose wage drift. The local negotiations, the annual revision of time-wages and the continuous process of negotiating piece-rates, offer opportunities to drift upwards in earnings. The ability to increase wages independently of the central union can be a factor helping to mobilize workers.[137] It may even be in the interest of the central union that there exists possibilities for wage drift; it gives meaning to the local wage negotiations and motivates workers to join the union.

LO has tried to implement its "solidaristic wage policy"[138] through trying to equalize wages for the same kind of work, and above all, to reduce wage differentials between those with the lowest and those with the highest wages. The reduction of wage differentials which can be accomplished through a solidaristic wage policy, is counter-acted through wage drift often pushed by better paid groups. When the central agreement increases wages for those with the lowest wages, wage drift often does the opposite, i.e. increasing wages for those with the highest wages.

Wage drift may also be valuable to the central organization. It may allow groups within the collective to reduce differentials to other groups in other worker collectives. The most valuable role may be its character of a free-zone. As it allows for "corrections" of the agreement, it may help to adjust the effects of the agreement so as to better coincide with traditional values at the work place. It may make a policy which is unacceptable for some more bareable.

Wage drift poses other problems as well. One of the ambitions of Swedish economic policy is to maintain the competitiveness of export industries. In order to accomplish this goal, a controlled development of wages is necessary. According to the "EFO-model", wages were to be kept below the increase of productivity and international inflation. Another target has been to maintain Swedish wage developments below those of its competitors. When productivity increases are small, and international wage developments are low, the room for Swedish wage increases is very much reduced. If wage drift remains on a normal level (it has not been below 2.3% even in recessions),[139] the room for centralized agreements is likely to be very small indeed.

If there is little room for increases in the central agreements one option is to prolong the agreement (zero-wage increases). This is hardly a sound strategy. A central organization which can not influence the development of wages may soon lose its legitimacy. Another option is to struggle for an agreement that would at least be on a par with wage drift. In this way, the central organization can play a part in wage determination, but contributes to the decline of industrial competitiveness. This would force the government to choose between a policy which restrains the economy and creates high unemployment or a policy of repeated devaluations which in the long term may prove harmful to the economic climate of the country.

Figure 4.1:    Wage drift and contractual increases

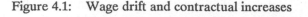
Wage increases, wage drift and contractual increases

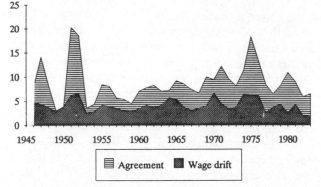

Source: SAF (1983), Johnston (1962), Martin (1984)

When wage drift reduces the scope of action for the central organizations, it decreases LO's or SAF's control over wage developments and jeopardizes LO or SAF as a bargaining partner with the government. These central organizations become less valuable for the government in the neo-corporatist bargaining that is a feature of Swedish society.

The wage drift of white-collar workers in the private sector has been low until recently. Their wage system allows a greater control over wages at the same time as the individualistic wage system offers a degree of flexibility. It is also of interest for some of their organizations to keep wage drift on a low level in order to gain control over their own wage determination, while others like CF are more positively inclined.

Traditionally blue-collar workers' wage drift has by far exceeded the wage drift of white-collar workers. It has been the aim of the TCO-unions to be compensated for blue-collar workers' wage drift. Wage development guarantees were developed in the collective agreements for white-collar workers in the private segment during the 1970's. The aim of these guarantees has been to reduce the influence of wage drift upon the wage differentials between different groups of employees.[140] Wage differentials in general and the design of wage development guarantees in particular, have been major obstacles in the wage rounds during recent years.

Blue collar workers' wage drift has usually been explained with variables from the labor market such as unemployment or various measures of vacancies. Labor market explanations often leave the social processes which lead to wage drift as a "black box". I will argue that blue-collar wage drift can be explained with other variables which focus attention on the plant level, in particular, on those processes and structures which feed wage drift.

In this chapter, I first present earlier research. Wage drift has mainly been the concern of economists, and earlier research has mainly tried to apply economic theories which focus on the labor market. Secondly, I advance the argument that pure labor market factors have relatively limited effect on blue-collar wage developments. I discuss research which suggests that the role of the labor market is often exaggerated.

My argument is: Blue-collar wage drift is a phenomena which can occur whenever less strict wage systems are used. Whenever the conditions of bargaining favor workers, employers with "loose" wage systems such as piece-rates may find it difficult to limit wage drift. The larger the free-zone, the higher wage drift. Thus, a rising business cycle increases the bargaining power of workers. Wage drift may originally take place in piece-wage settings, but is rapidly spread through social reference networks (communication networks or linkages among employee groups or firms in which wage comparisons are made) to time-wages and other more stable wage forms. When wage drift starts to accelerate in one industry which may experience a boom, export-driven or driven through internal developments, it spreads to other industries and companies through different reference networks where comparisons are being made. Companies have operational guide lines which lead them to follow the development of wages. They react to the information that is passed on through the social reference networks. Unions also have reference networks and may in local negotiations, force a development of wages which parallels that of other companies in the area or in the industry.

The methods used in this chapter have been several: At one level, interviews were carried out with labor market actors, this includes representatives of national unions, employers organizations, SAF and LO. As a part of the project "Löneförhandlingar i Sverige" interviews were conducted at five companies in the Uppsala region. In these companies the personnel manager, an LO-union representative and a TCO-union representative were interviewed. These interviews are documented in interview notes and in the working paper "A very preliminary draft of the Case-studies". I have tried to take examples from these case studies to *illustrate* my argument.

It is difficult to compare the Swedish concept of Wage Drift with occurrences abroad. Wage drift presupposes that there exists agreements that claim full jurisdiction over wage developments. If they do not, there is not any wage drift, only wage developments. It is therefore difficult to compare Swedish wage drift processes with wage developments abroad, since wage drift is not easily isolated in other wage negotiation systems. When discussing the causes of wage developments in the US, for example, what is being explained is both the negotiated wages and spontaneous wage developments. In contrast to international studies, there has been little Swedish interest in studying branch-specific patterns of wage developments. It may be useful to compare wage drift processes in Sweden with wage development processes in other countries, bearing in mind the differences between the systems.

# Earlier Empirical Research

There are two main lines of reasoning trying to explain wage drift. Many economists tend to see wage drift generally as a labor-market phenomena, others see wage drift mainly as the consequences of adjustments within the companies to changing internal or external conditions.

My argument is that it is possible to see these latter adjustments as responses to changes emanating from the product market. Changing conditions alter the power-balance of the actors. The bargaining power of the union is finally seen to influence the outcome: wage drift.

Several early studies on wage drift in Sweden all concluded that the state of demand and supply in the labor market highly influenced wage drift for blue-collar workers, and that the rate of unfilled vacancies appeared to be a better indicator than the rate of unemployment. Neither profits nor productivity were shown to have any significant effects.[141]

Other studies during the sixties and seventies found that the number of unfilled vacancies or other labor market measures were significant and dominating explanatory variables.[142] Among those who use non-labor market variables to explain wage drift are Dahlström (1969), Eskilsson (1966), Nilsson (1987) and various SAF and LO committees.

The first study of wage-drift was published in 1956 by Hansen and Rehn.[143] They started from the traditional model of supply and demand. They observed that, in the general debate in Sweden, wage drift had been regarded as the consequence of: 1) the scarcity of labor in full employment and of such factors as the increasing productivity of labor (which may increase earnings under piece-work rather automatically irrespective of the state of the labor market); and 2) the high profits of firms. (which may make employers more careless with regard to pay increases and employees more eager to take advantage of the wage-paying capacity of the companies) Their intention was to test the hypotheses that scarcity of labor, the profit situation, and increases of productivity under piece-work, respectively were responsible for the wage drift.[144]

Their model was tested on time-series data for eight branches of industry from 1947 to 1954. Their study indicated that the statistical analysis ought to focus on excess demand for labor and changes in productivity. Their conclusion was that wage drift seems to be conditioned by the wage systems applied and highly influenced by the state of demand and supply in labor markets. The development of excess profits seemed to play a minor role, and their material gave no support for the hypothesis that wage drift is an automatic consequence of increase of productivity in piece work, except in some industries where the wage system is most strongly tied to production results.[145]

Jacobsson and Lindbäck (1969) replicated the Hansen and Rehn study a decade later. Their explanatory variables were: The state of demand in the labor market, profits, and productivity increases. Their study showed that the labor market variable was highly significant, while the remaining independent variables were insignificant. A later study by Jacobsson and Lindbäck (1971) confirmed the findings, this time with data from 1950 to 1970.

The research up to this point had mainly dealt with aggregated time-series data. In a State Commission Report (SOU 1979:10) Schager presented a study of a cross-section of companies. The study consisted of around 60 companies for six time periods. The result was that neither the labor market variable, nor the profit measure could explain the wage drift that had occurred in the companies. He continued his efforts to find statistical models that would explain wage drift with data from individual companies, but did not succeed in finding any model which gave significant results.[146]

Schager (1981) later found in a time series study that wage drift for blue-collar workers in the private sector could be explained by the duration of vacancies together with a profit variable.[147] Schager's most recent model for wage drift analyzes firms' search behavior for labor. The variables that enter his model are the duration of vacancies, the stock of vacancies and the profit share of value added. He is able to present a model which seems to explain a great deal of the wage drift for the years 1964-1986 for Swedish industry.[148] Schager's model suggests that employers actively change wage levels so as to recruit labor.

Holmlund and Skedinger (1988) have made a study of wage drift in the Swedish wood industry. They employed a pooled design of 70 regions over the time period 1969-1985. Their starting point is a conventional model of wage bargaining. According to their model, wages are determined through negotiations between the firm and the local union, and employment is unilaterally set by the firm after wages have been decided upon.[149] They discuss three models, first a seniority model where layoffs are effectuated according to seniority within the firm. This model is expanded with two more sets of variables, first "envy" is introduced. The argument is that the worker's utility may decrease in the "reference wage", that is if somebody he compares himself with earns more money, he will also want to earn more. The third model incorporates the idea that the union acts in a utilitarian fashion, being concerned with the welfare of a group of workers including those who are unemployed. The union tries in this model to maximize the sum of the utilities of the employed and the unemployed workers.[150]

Their results give no support for the seniority model. Instead they find that outside wages and unemployment show up as significant determinants of wage drift.

The economic analysis of wage drift has been rather one-sided emphasizing labor market explanations, recently however, Nilsson has introduced the idea that norms are an important determinant of wage drift.

Nilsson's study (1987) of Swedish companies seem to confirm Reynolds' (1951) claim that companies and unions seem to utilize operational guidelines in wage negotiations. Companies aim at keeping their relative positions in the regional wage hierarchy, while unions aim at gearing agreements to national pattern bargains.[151] Reynolds found that the primary considerations of the managements were:

> ..(1) a widespread opinion that management is morally obliged to pay prevailing wages, and that inability to do so is a confession of managerial failure.; (2) a belief that failure to match wage increases made by other plants will lead to a lowering of employee morale and productivity; and (3) a belief that, over the long run, subnormal wages will hamper the company in recruiting a satisfactory labor force.[152]

Reynolds identified a number of reasons for keeping up with the wage level of "close"[153] companies. These are: paying a fair or ethical wage in order to minimize discontent, avoidance of unionization, and to attract an adequate quantity and quality of labor.

Nilsson (1987) found in his study that the local union and the company choose different reference points within the industry and the region. He attributes the rapid spread of wage drift to these comparisons. He suggests that wage drift is pushed forward in expanding companies by a need to recruit personnel. The wage drift which occurs in the time period between the application of central agreements, he attributes to negotiations over piece-wages at the companies.[154]

## Studies by the labor market actors

Economists within unions and employers organizations have conducted a number of studies of wage drift. They tend to stress other explanatory factors than those of the labor market. LO explains wage drift in structural terms, that is, wage drift does not mean increased wages, but is mostly a statistical illusion. The employer's organization in the engineering branch of industry (VF) studied the wage-drift phenomena during the fifties. They used survey-methods, conferences and committees to investigate the causes of wage-drift. Their conclusion was that wage drift was caused up to 75% by slack in the way piece-wages are set up, 10% by organizational and structural changes, 5% by unclear agreements, 5% by increased work-intensity and 5% by other factors. *Labor market competition is included in the 5% other factors.*[155]

### *Wage Systems*

The debate over the influence of wage systems on wage drift has gone on for quite some time in Sweden. Both LO and SAF have encouraged studies into these relationships. One of the most important mechanisms behind wage drift has been the wide-spread use of piece-wages in Sweden. Through piece-wage systems, it is possible to drift on wages in between local negotiations.

Wage drift as payments exceeding the centrally agreed upon wages will appear when there is an opportunity to re-negotiate wages. This is the case when a company use productivity related pay systems such as piece-wages. In a SAF-publication, Eskilsson (1966) distinguishes between primary and secondary wage drift.[156] Primary wage drift is the unintended development of piece-wages. Secondary wage drift is intended by the employers and is aimed at correcting the changes in the wage structure caused by primary wage drift.

Piece-wages are intended to cause variations in pay. Improved productivity is supposed to be rewarded through increased compensations. The problem is to discern the increased worker effort from other factors influencing the development of productivity. Primary type wage drift is an evidence of the lack of precision in this process. Dahlström (1969) reports that when new piece rates are established it may be difficult to calculate the rates in such a precise way that wage drift is eliminated. The work may not be sufficiently measured to develop reliable rates. Even if rates are not changed, there may be  wage drift because the work tasks change over time. Improved working methods may lead to wage drift if they are not followed up with adjustments of the rates.[157] When not enough attention is given to the setting of piece rates, or when rates are not adjusted when methods are changed, a gap is created between the performance that is judged possible, and the actual possible performance. A possibility arises either for wage drift  or  for systematic restriction of output. The level of wages and production is in fact decided by the workers.[158]

A time-study engineer may argue that wage drift can be eliminated if management keeps a close check  on piece-wages and revise piece rates often enough so that workers will not earn more on each job than the normal wage. The difficulty lies in enforcing what a displeased worker might experience as a "rate cut". It is difficult to prove that the increased earnings are a result of changes in methods rather than the increased effort of the worker. The worker may also have developed new methods which increase his productivity. Is he not to keep the gains from his ingenuity?

Reynolds argues that management hesitates to take any step that will diminish the workers' earnings. Rather than facing worker unrest they might prefer to live with a loose rate until the job is eliminated or the workers can be transferred to other work.[159]

Time-wages are not revised as often as piece-wages and have per definition no connection to the productivity of the individual worker. Nevertheless workers who only work on time-wages also experience a wage drift. But this is normally what Eskilsson (1966) call "secondary wage drift". When primary wage drift and contractual wage increases cause a change in the wage structure, *management may be pressured to correct this change in the wage structure*.[160]

A company may compare its wages with wages within the industry it operates in, with wages in other companies in the same area or with wages within the company itself. Industrial comparisons are made easy through the use of statistics which are provided by the employers association in cooperation with the labor unions of the industry.[161] Eskilsson claims that the influence of the local labor market is important in daily negotiations over piece-rates. Workers refer to higher wages paid by other companies in the same area. Time-wages are changed when the contractual wage increases are distributed, usually at least once a year. An important source of wage drift arises from the wish to even out differences between individuals and groups within the company.[162] In my own field study, two of the companies had even developed their own wage development guarantees. Time-wages were thereby increased automatically when piece-wages drifted.[163] Eskilsson claims that the companies accept secondary wage drift *in order to secure their position in the local labor market*, that is, they want to be able to recruit labor and to keep their labor force, although their fears may be exaggerated. This is the same argument as Reynolds made in his study of a US manufacturing town.[164]

## Characteristics of unions and companies

Internal SAF and LO studies have analyzed different possible factors behind wage drift; some of these are summarized here.

The LO unions are mostly organized on industrial lines.[165] Typically, all the blue-collar workers within a company belong to the same union. Workers performing the same tasks but in different companies may belong to different unions. This means that wages for a specific job task may differ between unions. If such differences arises, there may develop compensatory claims from those lagging behind. Central agreements may do violence to local wage differentials. Organizing unions along industrial lines may bring about different pay for the same occupation in different industries. If a driver receives a wage according to the "Fabriks" (manufacturing) agreement, he may compare himself with drivers who are paid according to the "Transport" agreement. He may then claim larger increases to be on a par with his colleagues in the Transport union.

Internal developments in large companies may affect the whole local labor market. Large complex organizations depend more on independent policies and rules which are likely to conflict with central agreements and therefore cause adaptations with wage drift as a consequence. Smaller companies may feel that they can not form their own independent wage policy. The small company is more dependent on a few key employees performing crucial tasks.

In markets which are protected from competition, it may be possible to pass on wage drift. If a company has only a few customers, the company may have a more difficult time passing on rising costs than if it has many customers. Eskilsson (1966) presents statistics for the period 1960-1965 which show that in industries without foreign competition, wages have drifted faster.[166]

LO has emphasized the structural part of wage drift. They argue that other unions should not be compensated for wage drift that is only the result of structural changes.[167] If workers move from companies with a low wage level to a company with a high wage level, this is recorded as a wage drift for that industry, even if the wage levels at respective companies stay the same. This is called the "Structural component of wage drift". Other structural changes may also be recorded as wage drift: changes in the number of Sundays, changes in the volume of piece-wages, changes in worker age structure etc.

While wage drift has been interpreted by economists as a labor market phenomena. it has to be acknowledged that it is a complex social phenomena. The pattern of wage drift differs between piece-wages and time-wages; wage drift may occur "spontaneously" or it can be the intention of management to allow or to encourage wages to drift. Managements and unions have operational guidelines for their wage developments. They make references to other companies and to the industry. The variety of factors that can nurture wage drift processes call for an analytical and critical discussion.

# A Critique of the Economist Approach

There are a number of questions which have not been answered so far. Although the labor-market explanation of wage drift seems to have some value in time-series studies of the whole of Swedish manufacturing, such explanations are less valid when disaggregating to the industry level, or in cross-sectional studies.[168] Despite the large changes in Swedish industrial structure, business cycles and the growth of the public sector, wage drift remains on the average 4% in the four epochs which were described in chapter two.[169]

It is also questionable whether the labor market operates like a market. Do workers consider wage differences as the decisive criterion for changing jobs? Do the workers have any alternative to changing job?[170] The development of administrative management of personnel decreases the importance of external labor markets. When recruitment is done more within a company and an employee can count on a long-term employment relationship, external wage comparisons may be less important for recruiting and keeping personnel. Holmlund (1984) has shown that quit rates in larger plants are below those in small plants.[171] Since large plants offer more potential for the development of internal labor markets, this indicates that the importance of external labor markets is diminishing.

If labor markets were well behaved in an economist's sense, the state of demand and supply for labor would influence the price, that is wages. It is possible to find such an empirical relationship when studying aggregate data for the nation. But the relationship is smaller or not significant in micro-level studies. If there develops a shortage in a perfect labor market, managements would find it profitable to raise wages to attract labor to fill vacancies. People who have not entered the labor market or who work at lower wages would then move to fill these vacancies and the balance would be restored in the market.

The argument that labor market supply and demand affects wage drift hinges on two presumptions: 1) that managers raise wages to attract more workers, and 2) that people are ready to move based on wage differences to these new opportunities. I will argue that there is little support for these presumptions. Instead I argue that managements work with a longer time-horizon and that there are other sources of labor power than labor market shortages.

## Does supply and demand in the labor market explain wage drift?

Is there a relationship between labor supply and demand on the micro-level? Schager was unable to find support for his labor market model of wage drift, when tested on individual companies in a cross-sectional study. The labor market explanation may be a case of a spurious relationships. Schager (1982) did not succeed in the cross-sectional study in finding any significant relationship between wage drift on one hand, and vacancies and profits on the other, nor did he succeed in showing that the duration of vacancies was sensitive to wage levels.[172] Since Schager finds the results difficult to explain, he suggests that there may be other "irrational" processes which govern wage drift. One explanation is that there exists a "demonstration" effect which leads companies to imitate the actions of other companies, thus spreading wage drift very fast, making it difficult to separate the different causes. He also suggests that there may be company specific processes, such as worker mobilization and specific wage systems, which may cause wage drift.[173]

Holmlund and Skedinger found significant effects of unemployment in their study of the Wood industry. A closer look at their equations reveals that the addition of the unemployment variables did not increase the explanatory value of the model. The increase in $R^2$ is, if all the entered unemployment variables are to be significant, less than 0.01. This indicates that the explanatory value of their model lies to a large degree in the introduction of "reference wages", which were operationalized as the wages in the industry and within the region in neighboring branches.[174] The link between supply and demand in the labor market and wage drift thus seems rather weak.

## Are Wages an Important Recruitment Tool?

What evidence is there that managements actively raise blue-collar wages in order to recruit more employees? The VF study mentioned in an earlier section did not consider labor market competition as an important source of wage drift.[175]

White-collar workers' wage systems are individualistic and secret. Wages are in most cases kept secret from other employees. A company can rather safely increase white-collar wages without upsetting the white-collar union. The blue-collar workers' wage system is on the contrary public, all wages are known to the other workers. If a company should unilaterally increase wages for a specific category of workers, this would in most instances be contrary to the solidarity norms of the workers. If a company wants to raise wages for a specific category of workers, this would immediately disturb the established norms around the wage system. Such a disturbance might lead to unrest and be difficult to handle. If a company wants to attract a specific category of workers with a higher wage, it finds itself forced to raise the whole wage level throughout the company.[176]

If the recruitment of personnel is not so much affected by wage levels, and if the tendency is toward maintaining the wage structure in the area, the source of wage drift has to be sought after in other places than the labor market.

While it may be necessary to maintain the niche in the area wage structure in order to preserve the quality of new recruits, it seems that incentives may be small to raise wages in order to recruit labor. In the five companies interviewed for this study, only one example of clear labor-market incited wage drift was mentioned.[177] Labor recruitment has a long time horizon. Maintaining wages on parity with other employers seems most important. A company tries to achieve a wage level which supplies the quantity and quality of labor which is needed for production. Only when people start to leave the company for another higher paying company does management increase wages substantially.[178]

Even if there is no perfect labor market, workers will have some knowledge of jobs other than that on which they are currently working. They may have some freedom of choice between employers and calculate the relative attractiveness of different jobs. Part of this calculation may be based on wage considerations. Workers will choose better jobs before poorer ones. Employers with attractive jobs will have a surplus of applicants while employers with less desirable jobs will encounter labor shortages.[179] *An employer wishes to retain a constant share of the area's labor force must keep the overall attractiveness of his jobs on a par with the attractiveness of other jobs offered by other employers.*[180]

One can regard the terms of employment in an area as an interrelated system. A change in any wage in the system must call forth appropriate changes in wages or in non-wage terms of employment in other jobs.[181] Rather than actively recruiting people through wage increases, it seems as if companies aim at keeping their places in the labor market.

## Do People Want to Move?

The economic model suggests that wage drift reflects the employers' ambition to recruit new personnel and keep the old. The question is how recruitment is affected by wage levels. Eskilsson (1966) argues from Swedish studies that the effect of wages upon recruitment has been overstated. First, studies have shown that wage differences must be in the order of 20% to be effective, that is to be an incitement for people to move.[182] Studies based on SAF's wage-statistics have shown that expanding companies do not have a higher level of wages or a more rapid wage development than companies which reduce personnel.[183]

Nilsson and Zetterberg (1987) have conducted a study on the wage structure and mobility of labor in Sweden. Their result shows that there is no correlation between the rate of increase in wages and the rate of increase of employment in a number of Swedish industries. In an international comparison, they found a positive correlation only for the USA. Their studies also show that the elasticity of the demand for labor depending on industry wage level has been decreasing in Sweden. That is, the employment effect of a change in real wages is decreasing. Their conclusion is that the Swedish labor market mostly functions on a push-basis. That is, people move to new jobs when they are pushed out from their old ones. Push-mobility has however not increased in Sweden to compensate for the lack of pull-mobility (or the recruitment of labor by higher wages).[184]

Holmlund (1984) estimated that movers during the period 1968-1974 on the average obtained about 4 percentage points higher real wage growth compared to a situation where they had decided not to move.[185] At first this may indicate that even a small wage differential is an incitement to move to another employer. A number of objections can be made: 1) The calculation is an average, there must be a number of persons who got higher wage growth and some who even experienced reductions in wages after moving. 2) Movers consist of both workers who quit voluntarily and those who are laid off. 3) Even though the relative wage was found to influence quit intentions in another of Holmlund's studies, he showed that when the material was divided according to sex, a strong effect was found for women, while the effect was not significant for men.[186]

Actual job changes in Reynolds study were not much influenced by the wage structure. He found that 66% of the people who changed jobs moved to jobs with a lower wage![187] Reynolds found no correlation between the rate of wage increase and the rate of change of employment in individual companies over the period 1940-1948. Reynolds' study suggests that the role of the labor market is exaggerated in the discussion of the wage determination process.

Following the internal labor market tradition, Åberg (1985) argues that the growth of internal labor markets diminishes the role of external labor markets. In the neo-classical model the external labor markets are given the principal explanatory value, while the impact of the administrative management of personnel is largely ignored.[188]

In an external labor market, wage differences are assumed to influence the behavior of employees. Workers quit jobs with low pay and seek employment in companies and professions with higher wages. Companies are assumed to differentiate wages within the company. If wages do not change fast enough according to changes in market conditions, the labor market will not function as well, which in turn will hurt social-economic efficiency.[189]

If the labor market is seen as a collection of units practicing administrative management of personnel, the rigidity of relative wages will not be seen as a major problem. The normal case will be that persons are employed for a long period in the same company. The recruitment of labor is geared toward young workers trying to find a suitable job.[190]

Åberg claims that the flows of workers between industrial branches, regions or companies are relatively small and that the necessary adjustment is done through the in-flow to the labor market. Young workers are drawn to expansive parts of the economy because that is where the jobs are. This takes place irrespective of pay differences.[191] His main conclusion is that the reduction of wage differentials during the 60's and 70's did not lead to a less efficient labor market, and that the importance of economical incentives for the mobility of labor has been vastly overestimated.[192] It looks as if people are not very keen to move, even if they are given higher wages. Also, the development of an administrative management of personnel counteracts the mobility in the actual labor market.

## Worker resources

Where are the causes of wage drift to be found? One may argue that workers possess resources which can be used to gain higher wages. Management is dependent on the cooperation of workers, especially in times of business booms. When profits are high, this will lead workers to claim their share!

Reynolds' US study showed that workers were sensitive to changes in wages at other companies, even if the actual levels were not questioned. If surrounding companies have given larger increases people will become discontented before they will start to leave, he argued. With discontent, the management may start to experience problems with morale and production. Reynolds writes:

> The problem which faces the employer who lags behind an upward wage movement is not mainly of labor turnover. Workers, particularly those who have several years' service with the company, will rarely leave for wage reasons alone. The problem is rather that they become increasingly dissatisfied *where they are*. Without quitting the job, they can make their discontent felt in the quantity and quality of their output and in their personal relations with supervisors.[193]

Hart and von Otter (1973) argue that the production efficiency depends on workers having either an instrumental or a normative orientation toward work. If such an orientation is missing, as is the case when workers dislike the wage system, and there are preconditions for the formation of a worker collective, then the preconditions for effective production cease to exist. Management is therefore forced to maintain a certain degree of consensus, otherwise they risk provoking strikes, obstructions, costly labor turnover and ultimately economic loss.[194]

When the disruptive potential increases, this is a resource for workers who bargain and in other ways struggle to raise their wages. Finlay (1987) claims in a study of the US West Coast Longshore industry that variation in wages or working conditions should be attributed to workers themselves and not to corporate manipulation.[195] Hodson and Kaufman (1982) criticized the argument that large firms "buy off" workers by paying them high wages on the grounds that this view diminishes the role of workers as active participants in the interchange with the company. They argue instead that in large firms, workers have resources that allow them to achieve their goals of improved wages and working conditions. Finlay found, in his study of labor practices in the West Coast Longshore Industry, support for the worker resource argument.[196] He summarizes:

> There was no indication of any conscious plan or design behind management's actions. ... The role of managers was defensive and reactive.

> Second, it is apparent that it was the workers to a large extent, and union officials to a lesser extent, who initiated the differences in treatment.[197]

The local union representatives that were interviewed in our study stressed the importance of having a united front of workers behind them in local negotiations. Only in one company with a very complacent union chairman could wage drift be directly attributed to management initiative.[198]

Earlier studies have had difficulties linking the development of profits with that of wage drift. This is due, in part, to a lack of understanding of the role of profits in the bargaining situation. It can be argued that the measure of profit which is of importance in local bargaining and in wage drift developments is *past* profits. Profits and especially extreme profits, may alter the normative climate so that worker militancy is increased and employers' readiness to resist wage demands is decreased.

Profit is usually interpreted in wage drift studies as an indication of a company's capacity to pay. I suggest that profit should instead be seen as having an effect on workers' mobilization and bargaining attitude. Workers and their representative may not be as well informed about the present profit situation as the management. What is known to all is past profits. Thus past profits should be of interest in a bargaining model of wage drift.

High profits activate a set of norms motivating workers to seek compensation. Profits are legitimate in a capitalist economy. It can be argued that they are a compensation to those who have invested in the company and therefore taken a financial risk. But very high or "excess" profits[199] are not tolerated in the same fashion, at least not in Sweden. There are laws against taking excessive interests on loans, and similarly employees and others may take offense at companies earning very high profits. In a zero-growth society, there is a finite amount of wealth. Anybody's profit must be another person's loss. In a small zero-growth society there may exist norms which force a redistribution of wealth. In a growth society, it is acknowledged that profits can be generated without anybody else loosing anything. But there may exist a level at which the feeling of being cheated may arise and re-distributive norms are activated. That is, high profits may then set in action a set of norms which demand a redistribution of this wealth. Both union leaders and management may be affected by this.

Howard and Tolles (1974) argue that past profits have a distinct influence on wage bargaining in the United States:

> Union leaders in pre-negotiation statements habitually stress past profits and associated indicators of past performance of the firm which they are about to negotiate -- naturally enough, since these are usually the only clues to the firm's future prospects that are available to them. Furthermore, the illusion that future wages can be paid out of past profits is cherished by much of the rank-and-file membership. Thus, past profits, regardless of their actual relevance to future ability to pay, become a distinct influence on union solidarity and hence on union bargaining power.[200]

They also argue that management has incentives to bargain on past performance records:

> In periods of business expansion, and whenever management expects to be able to raise output prices without a proportionate curtailment of sales, records of past performance will justify a conservative wage settlement.[201]

High profits may thus increase worker demands for pay rises, regardless of other economic circumstances.An example of consequences of this norm was the "excess profits" debate 1974 which led the government to pass a law forcing companies to allocate a portion of profits to blocked accounts, from which they could later be withdrawn for various forms of investments.[202] The unions wanted to restrict wage demands through some kind of government action, but the measures taken were not considered enough. Instead wages were to rise to unprecedented heights in the following years.[203] The level of profits is usually not known at the time it is created. Profits are determined in the yearly accounts of the company. Profits are therefore known only after the period when they are created.

High profits may then set in motion a set of norms which demands a redistribution of this wealth. Both union leaders and management may be affected by this.

*My argument is that product market developments affect workers' bargaining power directly, without being mediated through the labor market.* LO claims in a report to the 1986 LO-congress that inflation has its cause in price developments in product markets. From a study of 35 industries over the period 1970-1983, they found that the rise in demand occurred first in the sector of manufacturing which was open to international competition, mainly concentrated in mining, steel and forestry. After this first increase in demand for products, wage developments accelerated.[204]

There is some international evidence[205] that points in the direction of the product market as an explanatory factor behind wage increases. Mishel (1986) focuses on union organizational characteristics in the USA and concludes that:

> The results suggest that union wage gains are greatest where discretionary pricing power enhances employer's ability to pay and where unions achieve high coverage, practice centralized bargaining, and avoid union fragmentation. On the other hand, centralized bargaining provides no advantage in competitive industries.[206]

Mishel found that "the product market plays a significant role in union wage determination".[207] In a statistical study of US data, he found considerable effects for concentration and entry barriers. *A union production worker in a highly oligopolistic industry with high entry barriers enjoys a 16 percent wage advantage over a similar worker in a competitive industry.*[208]

The influence of product market forces on wage developments in the USA has been studied by Howard and Tolles (1974). They found that wage adjustments in a US manufacturing sector were more influenced by changes in product markets, as measured by profits, than by changes in labor markets. They further found that the wage change was influenced more by conditions in both product and labor markets in the years prior to the wage change than by the concurrent state of either of those markets.[209]

Navarro (1983) also argues that product market characteristics have been the most influential in determining union bargaining strength in the US coal industry. He says:

> First, the level of coal consumption has been shown to have been a major determinant of the swings in union bargaining power over this period, and industry profits have likewise influenced the power balance, although to a lesser extent.
>
> Similarly, the extent of coal stockpiling has been a significant determinant of the effectiveness of the strike as a bargaining tool ....[210]

Evidence of the importance of product market influence is also given in an article by Long and Link (1983). They found support for the hypothesis that product market power raises labor compensation. Concentration was found to increase wages and fringe benefits while decreasing voluntary labor turnover. Industry regulations which set minimum prices and restrict market entry, as in airlines, are estimated to increase hourly wages.[211]

Blanchflower and Oswald report their findings from a survey of 1,267 British personnel managers. The question which they were asked was: *"What factors influenced the level of pay decided upon in the most recent settlement?"*. The responses were grouped into thirteen classes. The most common answers were:

(i)   Profitability / Productivity.

(ii)  Increasing cost of living.

(iii) Going rate in the industry.

(iv)  External pay structure.

(v)   All the establishment could afford.[212]

Blanchflower and Oswald find it difficult to interpret these responses as favoring the competitive theory of the market for labor. Instead, they argue that the results support the insider-outsider[213] and bargaining theories of the labor market.[214]

Finally, there is evidence from Australia that over-award payments are mainly influenced by establishment specific sources of variation. Brown et al (1984) found that there was a substantial establishment-specific difference in 'overaward' paymęnts in all industries except in the construction and textile industry. Only in building construction was a strong occupation-specific difference found.[215] They wrote:

> The result suggest that, in most industries, one must reject the explanation of wage drift as primarily a phenomena brought about by the clearing of the labour market.[216]

Summing up: there is evidence from studies in the USA, Britain, and Australia that wage developments are linked to product market developments and structural conditions within the industry. This research suggests that local wage developments are influenced by factors affecting the vulnerability of the actors. Local wage developments would thus not only be a result of the clearing of the labor market.

In this section I have argued that the labor market plays a smaller role in the local wage determination process than has often been assumed. Studies of actual labor market exchanges show that very high wage differentials are needed to get people to move from their present job. The development of administrative management of personnel directs job changes to occur between positions within a company rather than between companies. Alternative explanations of wage drift can instead be found in processes which increase worker resources and bargaining power and also illicit wage comparisons and demands among worker groups. In the next section I will elaborate some of the ideas that have been discussed in this section and formulate a few simple models of processes affecting workers local wage development.

# Preliminary Studies and Models

The preceding section suggests that it would be useful to formulate models for the Swedish case, utilizing factors which do not emanate from labor market processes. The factors of concern here are: 1) those which concern the bargaining strength of the actors, and 2) the normative climate of the negotiations and the social reference networks in which wage comparisons between worker groups and collectives are made.

## Worker Bargaining Power

Wage drift fluctuates a lot over the business cycles. This variation has earlier mostly been ascribed to the influences of labor market competition. My argument is that these influences may just as likely come from the product market without being directly mediated by the labor market. Primary wage drift occurs mostly with wage forms such as piece-wages which are to a degree subject to workers control. Why should these rates go up in times of business boom? Factors other than those of the labor market vary with the business cycle as well. First of all, as business picks up, a company will increase its capacity utilization. At first this may be done without hiring of new employees. The cooperation of workers is needed in order to increase effort, work overtime, possibly going over to shift work and similar strategies. If wages are not consistent with workers expectations (which are partly formed through comparisons), then worker discontent may be visible long before any labor market changes are felt.[217]

My argument is that when workers become discontented with the company and its wages, this rapidly becomes expensive for the company. Before workers start quitting their job, they can make their discontent felt through reducing the quantity and quality of their production and in their relations with supervisors and management. The company may have contracted delivery clauses which entail considerable fines for failing to meet deadlines, if the company can not deliver, the customer has to turn to competitors instead so that the company loses in market shares. When business is good, shortages develop which make the problem acute. In such a situation it is wise of a company to allow wages to rise in order to maintain a good relationship with the workers. As the company is more sensitive to disturbances, labor bargaining power increases. At times when business is low, such disturbances are not severe, the company may have difficulties getting its production sold anyway.[218] Clearly, under such circumstances, labor bargaining power is low.

I suggest that labor bargaining power is a main source of blue-collar wage drift influences in Swedish industry! In the discussion below, I have tried to define bargaining power as an function of vulnerability. Bargaining power is a relational concept where one bargaining actor gains in bargaining power based on increased vulnerability of the other. The bargaining power can be used to improve bargaining outcomes, in this case, wages. I focus on employer vulnerability largely ignoring employee vulnerability.[219]

## Vulnerability

There are many circumstances which may affect the vulnerability of an actor. These circumstances can be used by the other actor to extract concessions and are therefore a source of bargaining power. Anything that makes the other party more vulnerable or oneself less vulnerable is useful in a bargaining situation. Vulnerability refers to the *consequences* of the actions of the other actor. In industrial relations, this usually means the consequences of actions which aim at reducing production (slowdowns, organized absenteeism, strikes etc) or at withholding pay (dismissals, lockouts, etc).

If the concept of vulnerability[220] is to explain wage developments, there has to be an actor who can exploit the vulnerability of the employers. Without such an actor, wage determination would be up to the employer.

The structural indicators of the vulnerability of the actors are divided into two groups: economic conditions and structural conditions.

Economic conditions:

a)    When the *demand for the product* increases, management becomes more dependent on the workers. In order to increase production, management needs the cooperation of workers. They may have to accept working over-time, changing work-schedules, even starting to work shifts. All such changes make the management more dependent on the cooperation of workers. Also, running a tight production schedule may involve problems with keeping to stipulated delivery dates, which in turn may involve possible fines. Indications of a large demand in the product market can be: high profits, high capacity utilization, a large stock of orders, low stockpiles of the product, and a low level of lay-offs in the industry. *Decreased stockpiling* within the company increases the bargaining power of workers. When stockpiles are low, there may be problems meeting delivery deadlines, which increases employer vulnerability.

b)    At low levels of *unemployment* and high levels of *demand for labor*, the workers become less vulnerable, since workers' alternatives for employment increase. High levels of unemployment and low levels of demand for labor makes workers more vulnerable.

Industrial structure factors:

> A *high capital/labor* ratio makes management more vulnerable to disturbances in production. In such circumstances a small variation in worker productivity may lead to a large variation in the value of the output. Management becomes more dependent on the cooperation and motivation of its employees.

> When labor costs are a small proportion of total costs, a wage increase will not be as important for the profits of a company as when the opposite is true. When labor costs are relatively low, top management interest in them may also be lower than would otherwise be the case.

## An Empirical Assessment of Vulnerability as a Cause of Wage Drift[221]

Wage drift is unequally distributed between industries. Wage drift also varies over time, differently in different industries. The highest average wage-drift occurs in construction, followed by steelyards. Low wage drift occurs in Textile and for drivers and warehouse workers in retail. The largest variation in wage drift occurs in the chemical industry and paper and pulp industry, followed by the construction and steel industry. Workers in the slaughterhouses and butchers have a pattern of medium level wage drift with small variation. This has resulted in a wage drift close to the average for the whole industry sector. Construction has the highest wage drift but has had the lowest average increase in income during the period.

The measure depreciation/value added has been obtained from SIND and indicates the amount of capital involved in the production process. The correlation between wage drift and depreciation/value added is 0.75 $p=0.03$. This supports the hypothesis that employer vulnerability, measured in the form of industrial structure, increases wage drift.

Table 4.1: Wage drift in Sweden, selected industries 1970-1979

| Industry | Wage Drift | | Depreciation/ |
|---|---|---|---|
| | Mean | SD | value added[222] |
| Construction | 6.6 | 2.9 | - |
| Steelyards | 5.8 | 2.4 | 15 |
| Chemicals[223] | 5.2 | 3.3 | 13 |
| Paper and Pulp | 5.1 | 3.3 | 17 |
| Engineering | 5.0 | 1.4 | 9 |
| Construction materials | 4.9 | 2.1 | 12 |
| Slaughterhouses and butchers | 4.8 | 0.8 | 8 |
| Sawmills | 4.8 | 2.2 | 7 |
| Wood-industry | 4.6 | 1.4 | 7 |
| Retail (drivers and warehouse) | 4.0 | 1.6 | - |
| Textile | 3.3 | 1.3 | 5 |

The hypothesis that employer vulnerability influences wage drift was tested on data from Swedish manufacturing (SNI 3) over the period from 1969-1983.

In this model we have one measure of the vulnerability of the management and one measure of profits. The profit variable is an indicator of the normative climate around the negotiations. The higher profits in the past years, the more will management under pressure to let wages rise. The "stock of finished products" variable is assumed to catch the vulnerability aspect of product demand. A variable has been added which measures the number of implemented agreements during the period.[224] The more implementations, the more occasions for wage drift in local negotiations. As can be seen a significant model is achieved.

Figure 4.2: A model of wage drift

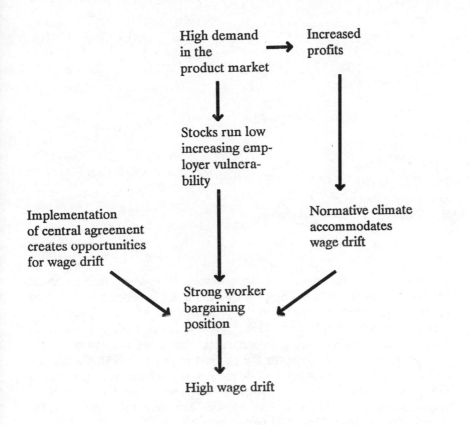

The regression equation is estimated for the period 1969 to 1983 with the least square method, t-values are given below the coefficients. F- and Durbin-Watson statistics (DW) are also given. The estimated equation is as follows:


| WD = | 3.37 | + 0.53 **PP** | + 0.62 **D** | - 0.066 **S** |
|------|------|---------------|--------------|---------------|
|      | (7.4) | (5.3) | (2.8) | (-6.3) |

N = 15        Adj $R^2$ = 0.82 F = 22.8        DW = 1.938


**WD** = Wage drift
**PP** = Past profits
**D** = Agreement effect
**S** = Stock of finished products


It would have been desirable to use a variable measuring unemployment or vacancies in the model. The problem is that there arises a high degree of multi-collinearity. It seems as if the profit and stock variables and labor market measures correlate to a high degree. It can be argued that there is a causal relationship between the variables. First there is a change in the product market, the demand for the product increases and stocks decreased while profits go up. After a while the boom will force managements to hire more people, and unemployment decreases while the number of vacancies increases. There are not enough data points in order to sufficiently separate the effects of labor and product market.

My interpretation is that we should not rule out that employer vulnerability and high profits lead to increased wage drift, at least under Swedish conditions. Even though the measure used covers both piece-wages and time-wages, which makes it impossible to separate the effect of the process on each wage form, it can be assumed that it is through piece-wages that the process mainly operates. The reason is that the adjustment on time-wages does not occur as easily. Since adjustments on time-wages mainly take place at the regular local wage negotiations, there is simply little opportunity to drift spontaneously. Piece-wages give an opportunity to continuously bargain about rates, and an opportunity for factors such as employer vulnerability and high profits to actually influence a factual decision.

## Reference Networks as a medium for the spread of wage drift

Wage comparisons are made with reference to some group or fact. Earlier research[225] has focused a lot on which groups people compare themselves with, who are the actual Joneses in various social structures, with whom people try to keep up? It is not the aim of this study to answer this, instead the focus is on structures, some of which may be institutionalized, which perpetuate these comparisons. Such structures may be called *Reference Networks*. A reference network may be a union with the information available to compare wages between different establishments. It may be a conglomerate which opens up avenues of comparisons between the companies within its control. It may be the cooperation between employers in regional employers associations. For individuals, their social network may become their reference network.

My focus is on networks which may help to spread such information and contribute to wage drift. When primary wage drift occurs on piece-wages, it is customary to compensate time-wages so that differentials are restored. Time-wages can also be raised before, so as to anticipate the wage drift on piece-wages. The question is to what level is the management going to allow wages to rise, and how high wages is the union ombudsman going to demand? This is where reference networks help us to explain what happens. I will investigate some of the reference networks operating in wage drift processes.

### *Conglomerates*

Within conglomerates the wages of several companies and plants are coordinated. Wage drift raises demands for justice which may press wages upward. Within a conglomerate, the wage developments in individual companies may be scrutinized more or less carefully. Conglomerates may take the form of industrial groups and of financial holding companies. In the latter case, we may suspect a less strong network of wage comparisons.

From our interviews we found one steel-mill belonging to an established industrial group. In this company the limits of local wage increases were decided at the conglomerate level, where established wage differentials were allowed to remain. In another company in a different industry, we found the same pattern.[226] In yet another company, this was not the case. The company was owned by a holding company and no references were made to wage developments within this conglomerate structure.[227] It seems as if the conglomerate structure in some cases forms an important reference network for both companies and unions.

## Union officials and their statistics.

Unions can not be counted out. Their job is to ensure fair pay and the same pay for the same job. In actual practice, they may have a greater knowledge about the market than anybody else. The following description is based on interviews with union ombudsmen in the Uppsala region.

There are many small companies who are not members of the employers' association. Their workers often want the support of the union ombudsman in their negotiations. In larger companies, the local union chairman conducts negotiations with the company. It is only when negotiations get stuck that the ombudsman is called in. But in smaller companies, the rule is often that the ombudsman conducts negotiations.

The ombudsman prepares himself in discussions with the "avdelning" representative at the company, if there is no local club. At the actual negotiations, he can argue that wages should be raised with reference to an average for the worker category, or compared to the wages in the region, or compared to wage-leading companies. In the last case, the ombudsman has to refer to hearsay. The wage statistics of individual companies are not officially available to him, so he cannot refer to these figures directly. There exists a rule in negotiations which states that all documents to which reference is made, should be available to the other side. Since he does not officially have possession of these documents, they cannot be referred to in negotiations.

When the ombudsman is engaged in negotiations, his knowledge of wage developments is far greater than the experience of the other participants. His strategy is most often to negotiate agreements that are close to those at other plants. It would undermine his position if he were to contribute to vastly different agreements. A union ombudsman who misuses his position may eventually undermine his possibilities in future negotiations. Trust takes a long time to gain and can easily be lost. The union "avdelning" keeps records of wage agreements and increases and can readily compare developments. The local union "avdelning" and its ombudsman thus become a reference network. In one of the interviewed companies, it was mentioned that when one company in the area practices straight proportional piece-wages, their wage development may come to affect a whole region.[228] When such wage developments are known to a wider circle, there is a motive for wage drift.

## Employer cooperation

There are a number of groups of employers in different regions who regularly meet and discuss wages and wage developments. The companies receive wage statistics from the employers' association to which they belong. These statistics may form a strong point of reference for the companies' wage policies.[229]

The spontaneous exchange of information on wages between companies seems to be very limited according to internal SAF studies.

## Official Statistics

Wage statistics are collected by SAF in agreement with LO and PTK. The companies regularly receive wage statistics from their employers' association. These statistics may form a strong point of reference for the companies' wage policies. From our interviews we find companies which try to keep workers' wages at 100% of the industry average as a policy.[230]

The difficulty in explaining wage drift at the company level may be the result of practices where the official statistics are used as a reference for wage developments. Wages are then not geared toward company specific targets, but to industrial averages, regional averages and so on.

## Orbits of Coercive Comparisons

Ross (1948) found that equitable comparisons played a central role in the transfusion of wage changes and wage rates from one agreement to another. The wage rates were however not uniform in local labor markets, let alone throughout the US.[231]

Ross identified a number of  orbits of coercive competition: labor market competition, product market competition, centralized bargaining within a union, common ownership of establishments, participation by the government, and rival union leadership.[232] These different settings refer to the bargaining between unions and employers. Some of these orbits are institutionalized in the Swedish system. Centralized bargaining as it has been practiced, has been a strong influence for the leveling of wages.

Centralized bargaining within an industry assures each employer an agreement which does not disturb the competitive situation.

Where wage drift is concerned, which is per definition increases above the agreement, factors influencing local developments are of importance. The orbits which may be of interest to us are those which do not entail centralized bargaining: local labor markets, product market, and common ownership of establishments.

Ross rules out labor market competition as an important factor. Product market competition he argues may spread wage decreases. Common ownership of establishment fuels the claim for "equal pay for equal work" within the corporate group.[233]

# Conclusions

Worker's wage drift has usually been explained with variables from the labor market such as unemployment or different measures of vacancies. The preliminary studies in this chapter suggests that wage drift can be explained in systematic studies using other variables which focus our attention on the plant level, to processes and structures which directly affects wage negotiations.

Hansen and Rehn's analysis indicated that the statistical analysis ought to be concentrated on excess demand for labor and changes in productivity. Their conclusion was that wage drift seems to be conditioned by the wage-systems applied and highly influenced by the state of demand and supply in labor markets.

Schager found evidence supporting Hansen and Rehn working with time-series data for Swedish manufacturing industry. He could not, however, replicate his findings working with cross-sectional data for individual companies.

The labor market actors have mainly concentrated on factors such as piece-wages and structural changes as factors behind wage drift.

I have argued that the labor market model fails to fully explain wage drift phenomena. First, actual hiring practices seem to be less dependent on wages as an incentive to recruit labor. Second, the increasing importance of the administrative management of personnel focuses on internal recruitment rather than on external recruitment. Instead the labor market seems to function as a norm to which employers and workers gear their ambitions.

The causes of wage drift should also be explored in dimensions such as product market conditions and changes in the product market that affects workers' bargaining power.

As I have suggested here, while wage drift may originate in one industry, it tends to spread to other sectors of the economy. Reference networks contribute to the spread of disturbances in the wage structure. Once an original disturbance occurs in the product market, wages are affected, and the disturbance is spread all over the economy. The construction industry is a source of wage drift "contamination".

LO-studies have shown[234] that price and wage developments start in the sector of the economy which is open to international competition, while the sector which is protected from competition (construction, food etc) lags behind. Evidence form our case studies and others[235] indicate that there is no reason to believe that wage drift occurs as an intentional process where management aim to retain its relative position in the local labor market. On the contrary, most often management mainly aim at keeping its relative position. Still, with an increase in wage drift in one part of the system, wage drift is soon spread throughout the whole system.

If one sees wage drift as the result of bargaining processes, several points can be made: 1) Profits play a role (and my preliminary studies suggest that past profits are important rather than present profits in such bargaining). 2) The influence of the business cycle operates through the product market rather than through the labor market. 3) Comparisons through reference networks shape the spread of wage drift. 4) Piece-wages are a vessel for wage drift by giving ample opportunities for bargaining over rates.

My conclusion is that workers utilize their bargaining power to increase wage drift if conditions are favorable and they are given the opportunity. In this process piece-wages are important. When sales boom, the workers bargaining power increases, this leads to higher wages through the continuous negotiations on piece-wages and through other wage systems which permit a flexible setting of wages. These wage increases are spread to other companies and industries through the pipes of the reference networks discussed earlier. The initial wage increase in a prosperous company is then spread over the entire labor market.

# 5   Expressions of Distributive Justice

## Introduction

In this chapter I shall argue that conflict between the different unions in Sweden is based on different rules or conceptions of distributive justice. The system of rules promoted by the organizations in their wage policies[236] will be compared with the principles espoused by their members.[237]

Principles of distributive justice play an important role in the determination of wages. Such principles are formulated in the wage-policies of unions and are used in wage negotiations at all levels of the wage bargaining system. At the central level, comparisons between different unions play an important role in the negotiation process. At the local level, comparisons are often made between companies.

Wage negotiations are rule-following processes also in the sense that some arguements are valid to be used in the negotiations while some are not. Wage-policies can be seen as such rules. These decide what principles can be referenced to in the actual negotiation and construction of an agreement. Wage policies are a kind of rules which can be used by the constituency to put pressure on the negotiators, at the same time as negotiators can rely on the wage policy of the organization to legitimize their position. Are these rules the inventions of the negotiators themselves or are they grounded in the opinions of their members? Are there differences between the different unions in the various segments of the Swedish wage negotiation system?

It can be argued that concepts of fairness are not given once and for all, but rather are shaped by the living and working conditions of people. What principles are then likely to emerge in today's society? I have investigated to what degree the different conceptions of distributive justice differ between different occupational groups. The dependence of world-views and class-consciousness on work-life conditions has been described by Lockwood (1975). He argued that workers' consciousness could evolve differently depending on their living and working conditions. Larger places of work, which are common in for example mining and shipyards, are expedient for developing 'traditional proletarian' world-views. On the other hand, smaller towns with smaller places of work such as agriculture, family enterprises, service occupations and craft jobs are likely to develop workers with 'traditional deferential' world-views.[238] Persons with these conceptions perceive social inequalities as status hierarchies. Lockwood thus suggests that workers may have two different world-views. It will be seen in the empirical analysis in this chapter, that this is also the case in Sweden. The world-view, or in this case, the conceptions of distributive justice, seem more contradictory for workers as a collective, than for other groups.

If such conceptions are dependent on work-life conditions, then it can be argued that in an capitalist society which is highly organized and structured, principles of justice which reflect this organization and structure will prevail.

What variety of principles of distributive justice is it possible to find? What is a principle of distributive justice? Miller (1976) defines social justice as the distribution of benefits and burdens through social institutions.[239] Social justice refers to the distribution of wealth and welfare which affects each and every member of a society. This distribution is the result of the rules followed by different social institutions, both private and public, such as government agencies, taxation, trade unions, private enterprise, health and welfare systems and many more.

Living in a society with limited resources, this means that everybody can not get their desires fulfilled, therefore social justice must be guided by distributive principles. Miller offers a definition of distributive justice:

> A genuine distributive principle must either simply recommend a division of goods, or else it must specify some property of the individual which will determine what his share will be. ... ...the most valuable general definition of justice is that which brings out its distributive character most plainly: justice is *suum cuique*, to each his due.[240]

This definition implies that equals should be treated equally. If their dues are the same, they should be treated the same way. This does not imply that distributive justice is subordinate to equality. Equality is rather one way of interpreting distributive justice which can be either accepted or rejected.[241]

One important feature of distributive justice is the differentiation it implies. Principles of distributive justice distinguish between people according to their characteristics. Equality is on the contrary a principle which refers to equal well-being, regardless of the individual's characteristics. Miller writes:

> I suggest that the notion of equality refers primarily to the end
> result -- the equal levels of well-being enjoyed -- whereas justice
> refers to the way in which each man has been treated -- namely,
> according to his peculiar needs and wants. This corresponds to
> the general conception of justice as *'suum cuique'*. Because 'just
> treatment' means 'treatment fitted to the individual', it also
> means in practice treatment which is different for each person;
> whereas 'equality' points directly to the identical levels of well-
> being which are the outcome of such different treatment.[242]

Principles of distributive justice are referred to when comparisons are made. Such principles can justify a differentiation of wages, why we are supposed to get more than the other group, why we are at all comparable with other groups.

Ross (1948) argues that comparisons are important to the members of trade unions. Not all comparisons are proper. In order for a comparison to play a role in union life, the entities being compared must show some similarity, they must be comparable according to some criteria. These criteria can be sought after in the conceptions of justice held by the members of the organizations, and in the wage policies of the organizations. These are rules or principles of justice.

Do the principles espoused by the members coincide with the principles promoted by the organizations? This is one question which will be investigated in this chapter.

# Wage Policies of Four Major Actors

Unions are organizations striving for their survival in an adverse environment.[243] In order to survive and grow, the leaders may have to change the goals of the organization. Michels (1915) argues that in order to increase their own security, the occupational participants modify controversial goals in the face of hostile environments. These goals may be seen in the case of unions as their wage policies. The interests of the union members are vast and varied. It is the task of the leaders to interpret the wills of the members and to reconcile their different interests.

We are here mostly interested in the wage-policies of the major union constellations in Sweden. The largest group is LO with 2.141.000 members (1981).[244] LO organizes workers in both the private and public sector of the economy. The other unions organize white-collar workers. TCO with 1.041.000 members (1981), is the peak organization for most white-collar workers, but does not negotiate about wages.[245] Finally SACO/SR must be mentioned. SACO/SR organizes 182.000 members (1981), mostly public sector employees with an university education, but it is also strong among technicians in the private sector. SAF is the dominating employers' organization in the private sector of the Swedish economy.

## LO's Wage-Policy

LO's wage policy is called the "Solidaristic Wage Policy". It has been formed through a long process reaching back to the 1920s. At the LO congress in 1922, the Stockholm section of Metall, raised the question of the large wage differences which existed between different groups of workers. They demanded that the LO developed a "socialist wage policy".

LO did not at that time have the statutory power to bargain for its member unions. This had to be remedied through a series of changes in the statutes of LO. This took place at the congresses of 1941 and 1951. The solidaristic wage policy got its present form at the 1951 congress. It combines egalitarian and political economical motives. The theoretical foundation was laid by the so called "Rhen-Meidner model" which claims that the standardization of wages and the improvement of wages in low-income branches of the economy will accelerate structural change in the economy and thereby improve productivity and wages in the long run.

The main principles of LO's wage policy are: 1) equal pay for equal work, 2) reduce wage differentials, and 3) differentiate wages according to principles acknowledged by LO. After 1965, LO came to emphasize the improvement of low incomes. LO has also tried to influence the wage development for white-collar workers so as to reduce the wage differentials between them and their own members.[246]

The fight against inflation became a "leitmotif" for the consolidation of LO. Before 1951 LO had no other options than to agree to wage freezes or let the unions loose in a free for all race for higher wages. There was no formula which could combine a wage policy which cared for wage injustices with economic stability. In the report to the 1951 LO congress, "Fackföreningsrörelsen och den fulla sysselsättingen", The economist Rehn argued that the state should take the full responsibility for economic stability. This should not be done through interventions in the collective bargaining process, but through the employment of indirect taxes. This would ensure that high wages could be extracted without inflatory consequences. The idea was to put pressure on companies to improve technology and rationalize working procedures.[247] The union should be responsible for keeping wage increases below the annual increase in GDP.

Wages should be balanced between different groups of workers. Wages should be determined less arbitrarily and more according to job evaluations. The main principle should be that equal work ought to be rewarded with equal wages. The existing injustices had led to compensatory claims which fueled inflation. Low wages also meant a subsidization of unprofitable companies.[248]

According to the report, the equalization of wages was desirable for two reasons. It was necessary in order not to jeopardize cohesion within LO. The second reason was that high wage demands in unprofitable companies would force an increase in productivity.[249]

LO as an organization has relied on the solidaristic wage policy as a rallying principle. The aim has been to ameliorate the position of those with the lowest pay. For this to be possible, LO has regarded the centralization of its organization as indispensable. The same process can also be seen the other way round. In order to expand and fortify the organization, the solidaristic wage policy has been the chosen instrument.

The solidaristic wage policy can be seen as a result of a union's "dialogical pattern of collective action".[250] In order to counter the comparably more powerful employers, the workers have to develop a collective strategy of conflict which not only aggregates the individual resources of the members of the organization, but also overcomes the individuality of those resources by defining a collective identity. The formation of such an identity deflates the standards according to which the costs of collective action are subjectively estimated.[251] The solidaristic wage policy can be seen as such a principle, it is not only a wage-policy, it is also an integral part of LO's entire strategy of conflict, a rallying principle.

In the report "Lönepolitik"[252] presented at the LO congress in 1971, the solidaristic wage policy was stretched out to encompass the whole labor market. The struggle for better wages for those with the lowest pay had previously been carried out within LO. With the advent of strong organizations among white-collar workers, comparisons between different organizations became more common. LO wished in the report to replace the relative low-wage concept with an absolute low wage concept.

The report "Lönepolitik för 80-talet"[253] presented at the LO congress in 1980, mainly confirms the position taken in the 1971 report. The 1981 report could look back at a decade of diminishing wage differentials. In it LO says that the solidaristic wage policy in practice has come to mean a reduction of existing wage differentials. It asserts, that this is not the principal idea behind the wage policy. Instead a lot more consideration has to be taken to the content of different jobs. The solidaristic wage policy means, in this rendition, that wages should be fair and just when the aggregated demands of jobs are considered.

Wage differentials continued to diminish in the 1980's. Many groups felt that the process had gone too far. It is not surprising that LO also should moderate its position. In the 1987 report to the LO assembly,[254] a tendency can be found which even more than before stresses that part of the solidaristic wage policy which allows for a differentiation of wages. The report stresses the importance of the solidaristic wage policy and coordinated negotiations for the cohesion of LO. Coordination, they write, is needed in order to come to an understanding within the union, about what principles are going to guide the development of wages. They continue to assert that coordination also has as a task the organization of democratic discussion about wage differentials. The solidaristic wage policy's task is, according to the report, to balance internal differences of opinion and group interests in such a way that lends legitimacy to the union.[255]

The goals of the solidaristic wage policy are now clearly divided into two: equality and justice. The core formulation for the solidaristic wage policy is still that wages should be fair and just when the aggregated demands of jobs are considered. But now the goal is clearly split up into two parts: 1) to decrease wage differentials across the whole labor market (equality), and 2) the same wage should be paid for similar jobs, and conversely, different wages should be paid for different jobs.[256]

LO still wants to compensate for the wage drift which occurs. The reason for this is that they want to counteract the influence of the market and to obtain improvements for those with the lowest wages. The compensation schemes in use have made it difficult to adjust wages for groups which have lagged behind in the development of wages. In order to make it easier to adjust wages for LO's members, the report argues that the whole of Swedish industry should be the base for comparison.[257]

It is clear that LO has mainly argued for a wage policy which can be called egalitarian. The aim has been to raise the wages of those with the lowest incomes. LO does not want the market to dominate wage developments, instead wages are to be put under human control.

## TCO: Solidaristic Wage Policy and Wage Differentiation

Unions of white-collar workers developed at a later date than was the case for blue-collar workers. TCO dates back only to the 1930s when the "old TCO" was formed. TCO as we now know it, was created through the fusion of "old TCO" with DACO in 1944. As a consequence, their wage policy is also of a later date than LO's. In 1961 TCO appointed a committee which was to examine the wage policy of the organization. In 1963 it produced a report "Lönepolitiken inom tjänstemannarörelsen".[258] Wages were supposed to be heavily differentiated, the aim was to raise salaries compared to the wages of workers. It asserted that white-collar workers should get compensation for increased costs and a development of wages which should be proportional to the rise in GNP.[259] A number of issues were deemed important:

- Equal pay for equal work

- A differentiation of wages according to the level of difficulty in the job.

- Differentiation of wages according to

    1) responsibility for operations, personnel and materials.

    2) theoretical and practical education.

    3) physical and psychic effort.

    4) inconvenient working hours and working conditions.

- Wage determination based on job and merit evaluations.[260]

The early wage policy of TCO scarcely referred to the problem of low wages, instead there existed a sympathetic bias toward the influence of market forces.[261]

Another wage policy study was presented in 1973, "Tjänstemännens lönepolitik" (TCO 1973). In it the principle of differentiated wages was reinforced. Now the emphasis was on the difficulty inherent in the job. The report also stressed the need for a low wage concept common to the whole labor market. TCO was now ready to distance themselves from market forces. They emphasized that the influence of market forces was to be limited, since these most often opposed the wage political ambitions of the union.[262]

TCO was to adopt a solidaristic wage policy in the 1970's. This differed from LO's mainly in its emphasis on differentiated wages. TCO's solidaristic wage policy meant: 1) equal pay for equal work 2) differentiated wages 3) improvements for persons with low incomes.[263] One difference between LO and TCO is that the demand for qualification in the work tasks show a wider spread among TCO's members. Different kinds of job evaluation schemes have been developed at an earlier stage than within LO. The wage policy of TCO was not decisively changed at the 1985 TCO congress. In the report to the congress it was suggested that wages should be differentiated should be based on the productivity of the employee.[264]

In the report from the SIF-commission "LP-75" TCO's wage policy is endorsed. They stress the importance of the difficulty of the job as a basis for the differentiation of wages. This difficulty factor is interpreted as: Responsibility for personnel, equipment and capital, plus the kind of work tasks necessary for the job and skill.[265] SIF also endorses the solidaristic wage policy as it was formulated by TCO.[266]

White-collar workers in the municipalities negotiate together within the cartel "KTK". KTK endorses the solidaristic wage policy, acknowledges the need for differentiation but leaves the decision up to its member unions as to how this differentiation is to be achieved.[267]

## SACO/SR: Wage Differentiation According to Education

SACO/SR calls their wage policy an "incomes policy". This is because they concentrate on income after tax and subsidies. Since income taxes are high in Sweden, a large part of well paid SACO/SR's members' wages disappear as taxes. Their disposable income then differs, in the eyes of SACO/SR, only slightly compared to other groups.

The differentiation of wages should according to SACO/SR depend on the following factors:

- The level of difficulty connected with the tasks.

- Long and qualified education should lead to higher wages.

- Experience

- Leadership and other forms of responsibility

- Working conditions

- Initiative and judgment.[268]

SACO/SR is opposed to the solidaristic wage policy. They acknowledge the principle of equal wage for equal work. In their interpretation this means that wages in the public sector should conform to those in the private sector of the economy. Otherwise they claim that wage differentials are too small.[269]

Particularly the unions in the public sector have stressed responsibility as an important criterion for differentiation of wages. In the private sector of the economy the principles of reward according to responsibility and capability have been stressed.[270] Here we find a wage policy with more emphasis on differentiation and less on egalitarian practices.

## SAF: Market Forces and Wage differentiation

The only available wage policy document from SAF is the document "Rättvis lön - lönepolitiskt program".[271] SAF stresses the importance of market forces for its wage policy. In some areas there exists a lack of workers while in others there is an over-supply. The wage policy has to ease adaptation in the labor market.[272] SAF also wants the managements to be able to adjust the wages individually for each employee. Each person is to be judged according to his contribution to the production process. SAF is opposed to the solidaristic wage policy. Instead SAF wants even more differentiated wages. The differentiation should have as its base the individual's contribution, capability and the difficulty associated with the tasks.[273]

There have been three conflicting wage-policies active in the Swedish wage negotiation system. The employers have considered the individuals contribution as the basis for negotiations while LO has stressed a redistribution in favor of blue-collar workers with low wages and TCO has striven for unchanged differentials. The consequence has been that TCO unions have tried to compensate themselves for the wage drift of blue-collar workers, while LO has regarded TCO's compensations as being based upon the wage increases awarded to those with the lowest wages. One effect of the introduction of wage development guarantees by LO in 1966 was to legitimate the relativity thinking of Swedish unions.

# The Distribution of Principles among the Population

It was our intention to investigate popular support for a number of principles which can be found in the wage policies of Swedish unions. SIFO interviewed in 1984 a cross-section of the Swedish population about, among other issues, their preferences for principles of wage distribution. What I was interested in was to what extent these principles were founded in the opinions of people having different occupations and belonging to different labor market organizations. A representative sample of 988 persons were interviewed. The response rate was estimated at 75%.

## The Questions Asked

The subjects were to take a stand on six different principles for distributing a hypothetical wage increase. They were to decide what principle they thought was the most proper,[274] which was the second most proper, and which was the least proper principle. The wording of the question excluded the concept of justice, this made it possible to answer the questions in a way that could be biased toward oneself.

The principles were:

1)  **Reduce wage differentials.** This principle was aimed to capture one aspect of the solidaristic wage policy.

2)  **All should have the same percentage increase.** This principle is a status quo solution. Wage differentials are preserved.

3)  **Give more to those with more responsibility.** Responsibility is, as has been shown, a cornerstone of the wage policy of white-collar workers. In their nomenclature, responsibility means having subordinates, that is, it is used synonymous with hierarchical level.

4)  **Give more to those who have produced more during the same working time.** This principle was supposed to reflect the legitimacy of piece-wages and the recent emphasize on productivity related wages among white-collar workers.

5)    **Give more to those with a higher education.** This is the main idea behind SACO/SR. They argue that as a compensation for the cost of education, people should receive higher wages.

6)    **Give more to those who have worked a long time in the organization.** This principle of seniority lies in the background of many wage policies. It is also a principle which has been used by local LO-unions when trying to implement the recent differentiation clauses in their agreements.

I did not include all the prevailing principles. Those chosen were however principles central to several unions. The wording of the questions was intended to replicate the wording of the wage policies of the unions themselves. Therefore the concepts are not strictly defined.

The principles in the study can be divided into two groups: those which differentiate among persons according to some characteristic of the person or of the job-task, and those which do not. The first group are differentiating principles, while the others are non-differentiating principles. The differentiating principles can further be divided into two groups: those which concern performance and job tasks, and those which concern the merits of the individual person. In the following presentation, the performance oriented principles ("responsibility" and "to those who have produced more" will be called differential principles, while the other differentiating principles ("education" and "seniority") will be left out of the analysis. The principles "reduce wage differentials" and "same percentage increase"[275] are called non-differential principles.

## Support for the Responsibility Principle

The most striking result of the investigation was the strong support for the responsibility principle, 38% of the respondents said that this was the most proper principle. Even though the support was stronger among white-collar workers (TCO 45%, SACO/SR 48%) it was the most widely supported principle among LO-members as well (29%).

The principles which approached responsibility in importance were those which expressed differing degrees of egalitarianism.

Figure 5.1:    Union members opinion of the principles

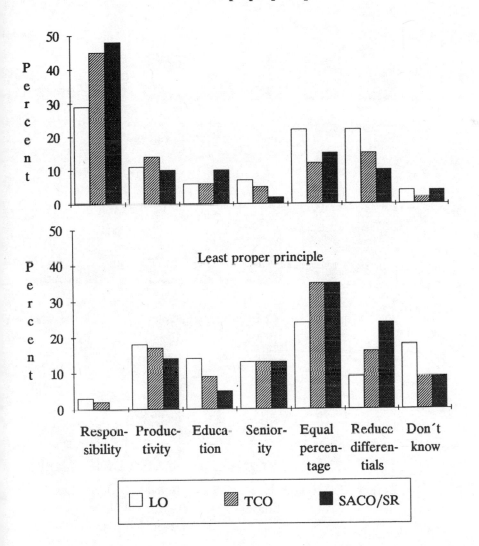

Figure 5.2:   The Swedish population's opinion of the principles

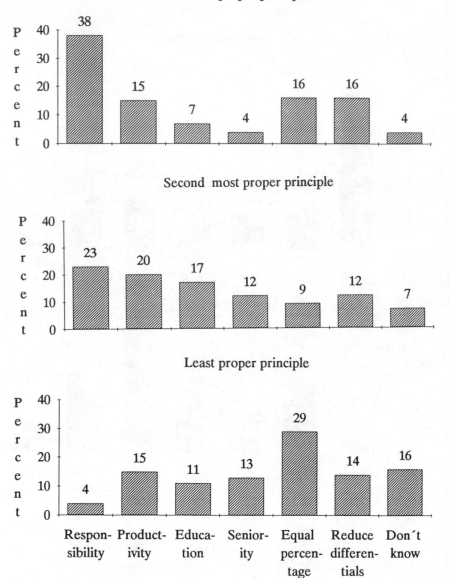

Table 5.1:    LO-members according to training

| Training | Differentiating principles most proper | Non-differentiating principles most proper | Don't know + other | | N |
|---|---|---|---|---|---|
| A few weeks | 37% | 52% | 11% | 100% | 87 |
| < 1 year | 38% | 41% | 21% | 100% | 81 |
| 1 - 2 years | 38% | 49% | 14% | 100% | 31 |
| > 2 years | 48% | 37% | 15% | 100% | 81 |

Table 5.2:    LO-members according to training, wage differentials at the work-place

| Training | Too small | Proper | Too large | Don't know | % | N |
|---|---|---|---|---|---|---|
| A few weeks | 6% | 45% | 37% | 18% | 100% | 87 |
| < 1 year | 5% | 55% | 38% | 2% | 100% | 81 |
| 1 - 2 years | 13% | 47% | 20% | 20% | 100% | 31 |
| > 2 years | 12% | 40% | 27% | 21% | 100% | 81 |

## Non-differentiating principles

The most clearly non-differentiating principle, the principle of decreasing differentials, has a fairly strong support, 16% of the respondents found this the most proper principle. The other principle, "all should have the same increase in percent" gets the support from the same number of persons 16%. There are however more respondents (29%) who think this was the least proper principle. Both principles may be viewed as non-differentiating, since they do not aim to differentiate among people according to personal characteristics.

## LO-members

The strongest support for non-differentiating principles was found among LO-members. 44% of LO-members thought that these principles were the most proper.

Support for non-differentiating principles is not uniform within LO. We found that skilled workers (with tasks which needed more than two years of training) were significantly more inclined to support differentiating principles. (See table 5.1) They also consider the wage differentials at the working place too small to a larger degree than unskilled workers. (See table 5.2)

Support for differentiating principles is strong among LO members employed in the private sector, 51% thought those principles were most proper. (See table 5.3)

Although support for the non-differentiating principles is strongest among LO members, it is not uncontested. 29 % of LO's members support the responsibility principle as their most proper principle, and 33 % thought the non-differentiating principles to be the least proper ones. (See figure 5.1)

It is of course not possible to draw a final conclusion about support for LO's solidaristic wage policy. The policy is as has been shown, built around partially conflicting goals: both equalization and differentiation. None of the questions were directly aimed at capturing the solidaristic wage policy. But what we can see is that there exists only a limited support for further reductions of wage differentials and that many LO members support differentiating principles.

Table 5.3:    LO-members working in private or public sector

| Sector | Differentiating principles most proper | Non-differentiating principles most proper | Don't know + other | | N |
|---|---|---|---|---|---|
| Private | 51% | 40% | 9% | 100% | 149 |
| Public | 29% | 48% | 23% | 100% | 137 |

The picture which emerges conforms to the one given by Offe when he claims that the working class is more vulnerable than other groups to distortions in the way which they conceive society. It is also consistent with Lockwoods findings. The LO members are split between two different world views: one egalitarian and the other competitive.

## White-collar workers

The most ardent supporters of the responsibility principle were to be found among white-collar workers. Both TCO and SACO/SR members supported the principle to a large extent. 45% of TCO members and 48% of SACO/SR members gave their support to this principle. (See figure 5.1) They also considered to a large extent that the non-differentiating principles were the least proper. (TCO 51% and SACO/SR 59%) Only a few of their members considered the differentiating principles to be the least proper. (TCO 19% and SACO/SR 14%) From this the conclusion can be drawn that there is a larger consensus among the members of TCO and SACO/SR about what principle should be used than within LO.

Table 5.4:        Union members: most proper principle

| Union | Differentiating principles most proper | Non-differentiating principles most proper | Don't know + other | % | N |
|---|---|---|---|---|---|
| LO | 40% | 44% | 17% | 100% | 286 |
| TCO | 59% | 27% | 13% | 100% | 213 |
| SACO/SR | 58% | 25% | 16% | 100% | 35 |

Table 5.5:        Union members: least proper principle

| Union | Differentiating principles least proper | Non-differentiating principles least proper | Don't know + other | % | N |
|---|---|---|---|---|---|
| LO | 21% | 33% | 45% | 100% | 286 |
| TCO | 19% | 51% | 31% | 100% | 213 |
| SACO/SR | 14% | 59% | 27% | 100% | 35 |

## Differences between the Sectors of the Economy.

The respondents were divided by SIFO into the categories "blue-collar workers" and "white-collar workers". When we compare those who work in the public sector with those who work in the private sector, we find the following:

Table 5.6:       Blue-collar workers / white-collar workers
                 public/private sector: Most proper principle

| Blue/white collar<br><br>Publ./priv. sector | Differen-<br>tiating prin-<br>ciples most<br>proper | Non-differen-<br>tiating prin-<br>ciples most<br>proper | Don't<br>know<br>+ other | % | N |
|---|---|---|---|---|---|
| Blue-collar Workers<br>public sector | 34% | 45% | 21% | 100% | 157 |
| Blue-collar workers<br>private sector | 52% | 38% | 10% | 100% | 176 |
| White-collar workers<br>public sector | 56% | 28% | 16% | 100% | 158 |
| White-collar workers<br>private sector | 71% | 21% | 8% | 100% | 156 |

Table 5.7:       Blue-collar workers / white-collar workers
                 public/private sector least proper principle

| Blue/white collar<br><br>Publ./priv. sector | Differen-<br>tiating prin-<br>ciples least<br>proper | Non-differen-<br>tiating prin-<br>ciples least<br>proper | Don't<br>know<br>+ other | % | N |
|---|---|---|---|---|---|
| Blue-collar workers<br>public sector | 21% | 25% | 54% | 100% | 157 |
| Blue-collar workers<br>private sector | 20% | 35% | 45% | 100% | 176 |
| White-collar workers<br>public sector | 21% | 48% | 31% | 100% | 158 |
| White-collar workers<br>private sector | 9% | 58% | 33% | 100% | 156 |

The largest support for non-differentiating principles was found among blue-collar workers in the public sector. There 45% supported these principles. The support was least and the opposition most among white-collar workers in the private sector (21% favored non-differentiating principles while 58% disliked them) (See table 5.6 and 5.7)

The largest support for the differentiating principles was found among white-collar workers in the private sector (71% favored differentiating principles).

A similar pattern was discovered for the question about wage differentials at the work place. The largest proportion of those who thought the differentials were too large was found among public sector blue-collar workers (37%), while the largest proportion who thought the differentials were too small was found among white-collar workers in the same sector (14%).

The opinions of employees in the private sector differed insignificantly from each other. (See table 5.8)

Table 5.8:    Blue-collar workers and white-collar workers, private and public sector: wage differentials at the work-place

| Blue/white collar Publ./priv. sector | Too small | Proper | Too large | Don't know | % | N |
|---|---|---|---|---|---|---|
| Blue-collar workers public sector | 8% | 47% | 37% | 7% | 100% | 157 |
| Blue-collar workers private sector | 7% | 57% | 24% | 12% | 100% | 176 |
| White-collar workers public sector | 14% | 51% | 26% | 9% | 100% | 158 |
| White-collar workers private sector | 8% | 61% | 20% | 10% | 100% | 156 |

Table 5.9:        Union members wage differentials at the work-place

| Union | Too small | Proper | Too large | Don't know | % | N |
|-------|-----------|--------|-----------|------------|-----|-----|
| LO | 8% | 51% | 33% | 8% | 100% | 286 |
| TCO | 7% | 57% | 28% | 8% | 100% | 213 |
| SACO/SR | 20% | 43% | 24% | 13% | 100% | 35 |

## SACO/SR and education

SACO/SR is a union which bases membership on the level of education. This union organizes mostly members with university level higher education. It is, therefore, no surprise that their members support the "education" principle to a higher extent than the members of other unions. But it is also worth to notice that the support is rather small: only 10% of the SACO/SR members support the principle while 6% of the other unions' members support the same principle.

## Desert and Compassion

It seems as if the principles of distributive justice according to desert and compassion with those with low pay are fundamental values in the Swedish wage bargaining system.

The interesting fact is that responsibility should be the differentiating criteria, rather than for example performance. One could argue that the performance principle is more in line with a more pure market society. The education principle is not seen as very important either. Responsibility is however a natural choice in a highly organized society. .

As more people work in large hierarchies, where external labor markets are exchanged for rule systems of administrative management of personnel, hierarchical concepts of distributive justice become more important. The growth of the public sector has also contributed to the creation of hierarchical work places which are unaffected by market forces

Figure 5.3:    Public consumption as a percentage of GNP

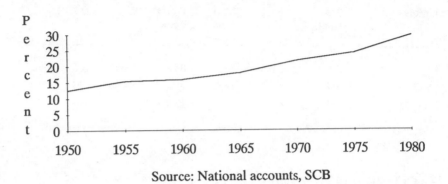

Source: National accounts, SCB

Source: SCB (1982)

The concentration of capital in Sweden has also meant the creation of larger places of work and larger organizations. In 1982, 77.6% of the employees of SAF member companies were employed in companies with more than 50 employees.[276] But the concentration of capital results in bringing many of these companies under a single ownership.

As a result, a person is less and less a commodity in a labor market and more and more an organizational cog. Hedström (1986) has shown that much of the variation of wages in Swedish industry is explained by components internal to the enterprises. He also finds support for the hypothesis that wage differentials can be explained by the number of hierarchical levels and the span of control.[277]

The increasing importance of rule systems for the administrative management of personnel have also decreased the "market character" of employment. The employment relation is relatively stable. Over 50% of an individual's employment time is expected to be spent in employment relationships which last for 20 years or more.[278]

Support for egalitarian principles is a characteristic of traditional proletarian workers, while support for responsibility and performance is more characteristic of traditional deferential and privatized workers. It seems also to be consistent with Miller's thesis that blue-collar workers should show more contradictory values. We find that 44% of LO-members support egalitarian principles, while 40% support principles based on distributive justice according to desert. TCO-members are more consistently for differentiating principles (59%), while fewer support egalitarian principles (27%). (See table 5.4 and 5.5)

Table 5.10:    Expected duration of the present employment relationship in the career. Age group: 30-34 years.

| Years | 1968 | 1974 | 1981 |
|-------|------|------|------|
| 0-5   | 4.6% | 2.9% | 2.6% |
| 6-10  | 18.1% | 15.4% | 13.1% |
| 11-15 | 13.3% | 17.2% | 16.0% |
| 16-20 | 15.7% | 11.1% | 17.5% |
| 21-25 | 18.0% | 18.7% | 13.7% |
| 26-30 | 19.2% | 15.5% | 14.2% |
| 30-   | 11.1% | 19.0% | 22.8% |
|       | 100% | 100% | 100% |

Source: Korpi and Åberg 1985.

If we control for income, we find that income has no effect upon blue-collar workers values, while it has a marked effect on other employees values. An interpretation is that hierarchy is not coupled to wages for blue-collar workers to the same extent as for white-collar workers. On the other hand, if wages for blue-collar workers are dependent on levels of hierarchy, which Hedström's data suggest, then the support for differential values among blue-collar workers cannot be explained by the blue-collar worker's position in the hierarchy. Other factors, such as the size of the work-place, the structure of the community etc. may be influential.

Figure 5.4:        Support for principles, depending on income and
                   union membership.

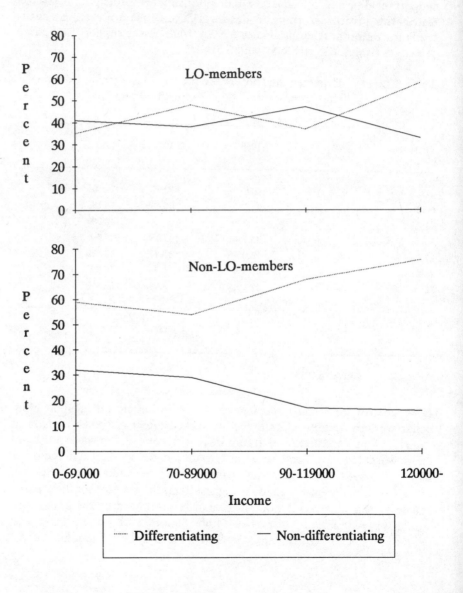

# Competition between Unions

Ross (1948) argues that comparisons are important to the members of trade unions. They establish the dividing line between a fair deal and being cheated. The worker knows that he cannot demand too high a wage, but he wants an equitable wage, he wants what is coming to him. In a competitive society such as ours, it is an injury to his dignity and a threat to his prestige to receive less than another worker with whom he can legitimately compare himself.[279]

The need to evaluate their leaders emerges among the members. How is this done? There are basically two ways: 1) to compare actual results with the goals of the organization. 2) to compare the results with other unions. As long as the organizations have different goals, comparisons between them may be difficult to handle.

Comparisons are important in the union world. They measure whether a union has done as well as another. They show whether the bargaining committee has done a good job, whether the member gets his money's worth for his dues. A favorable comparison becomes an argument for the re-election of union officers, helps recruit members and offers an occasion for advancement within the union hierarchy. An unfavorable comparison may threaten the survival of the union as dissatisfied members may revolt, elect new leaders and open up an opportunity for rival unions to enter the territory.[280]

Table 5.11:    Wage differentiation: blue-collar workers, white-collar workers Index 1972 = 100

|  | 1972 | 1976 | 1979 | 1980 |
|---|---|---|---|---|
| All | 100 | 89 | 87 | 88 |
| Within group differentiation | 100 | 81 | 76 | 79 |
| Between group differentiation | 100 | 100.1 | 101.8 | 99.6 |

Source: SAF: Lönespridning arbetare tjänstemän 1972-1980, 1981

At the central level, there is a fierce competition between the different unions about the distribution of the National Income. LO has tried to reduce differentials between blue-collar workers and white-collar workers, while the TCO unions have resisted any such attempt. At the same time each group has achieved a reduction of differentials within their own ranks.

Blue-collar workers in the private sector enjoy considerable wage drift, which until recently was out of reach for white-collar workers in the private sector. Wage drift has as an effect to reduce the difference in wages between white-collar workers and blue-collar workers. White-collar workers therefore have to be compensated in the central negotiations in order to restore the differentials. The same is true for employees in the public sector, their rigid wage system effectively controls wage drift and thus forces them to compensate in central negotiations to retain the status quo.

LO has as their ambition to raise the wages of those with the lowest income. The obstacles which LO faces are two-fold.

1)    LO organizes those with the lowest wages in the economy. If wages were to be raised for them, without sacrifices from other groups within LO, LO's share of the room for wage increases would have to be larger. This would entail getting a higher percentage wage increase than other unions.

2)    Within LO there are groups which have a largely independent wage development. Through wage drift, construction workers, for example, have been able to maintain high wages. But as the wage drift is recorded, this reduces the room for increases for those with low wages. Other groups in the economy also want compensation for wage drift within the LO-collective.

The white-collar workers' unions organize many persons with high wages. The cost for raising low wages will therefore be spread over a larger wage sum, and the consequences will not be as large in percentage terms. White-collar workers face another problem: their wage system is relatively more rigid and therefore their wage drift has been smaller until recently.

Figure 5.5:    Wage drift

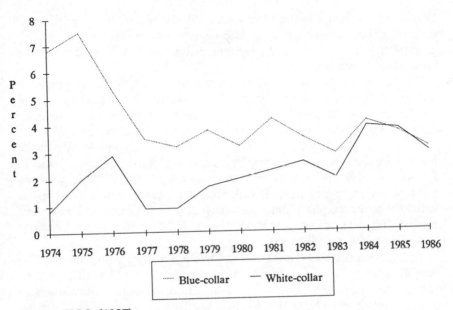

Source: TCO (1987)

The white-collar workers have had to negotiate special increases to keep pace with the wage drift of blue-collar workers. There exists also a sensitivity about differentials among white-collar workers. Foremen, who are organized in SALF, try to maintain a "distance of respect" to the workers they supervise. Likewise, SACO/SR tries to maintain wage levels which are higher than other groups.

The number of persons with low wages also differs between the sectors of the economy. In the state sector there are relatively few persons with low wages. The cost for raising low wages will be comparably lower than for the municipalities, where the number of persons with low wages is larger.

As we have shown, the opinions of the members of each organization tend to be reflected in the organization's wage policy. LO is the organization with the most "radical" members, but it is also the organization which has the greatest diversity of opinions among its members.

## Principles of Distributive Justice under Organized Capitalism

Organized capitalism is the term Miller (1976) uses to describe the new form of market societies. The growth of large enterprises and the demise of entrepreneurs creates a new system in which markets do not play as large a role as earlier.

In this system the workers bargain through unions with the employer and are thus not so directly exposed to market forces. Other groups of employees have obtained a career pattern of employment, security of tenure, regular promotions etc. The main effect of this change is that the exchange relationship i.e. markets, have declined in importance while membership of a corporate group becomes the new increasingly significant factor. This new society is moving away from a stress on individualism to an emphasis on organization. It resembles the hierarchical order of feudal society with its emphasis on  hierarchy of status, power and economic reward. But it believes that each person should be placed in the hierarchy according to his capacity and talent.[281]

What is presented here is a micro-rendition of corporative society. The emphasis is not on cooperation between management and workers, but on the fact that society is dominated by a number of large organizations to such an extent as to become what Miller calls an 'organization of organizations' rather than a society  of individuals.

In the individualist society, he argues, the principle of desert was taken care of by the operation of the market; each man was seen as an independent producer of goods or supplier of services. Desert refers to the justification of rewards on the basis of specific qualities and actions of individuals. The basis for desert are personal characteristics of individuals which are met by appraising attitudes. Desert is a reward rather than an incentive.[282] In an organized society, each person is seen as a member of a corporate group which collectively produces goods and services, or according to the concept introduced in this thesis: the person is not evaluated according to anonymous market forces, but according to principles in a rule system, an administrative management of personnel.

Miller argues that it becomes difficult to isolate and measure each person's desert. Instead each position is graded according to the contribution to the final product they make, and then persons are evaluated competitively so as to fit into these positions.  These organizations have goals which aim to make contributions to the community. Here we have now a reconciliation of the principles of desert and need: desert being manifested in the fulfillment of a function which helps to satisfy the needs of others. This solution has a strong moral appeal.[283] But there is a tension within the ideal: It is not clear what importance is to be placed upon desert and need.

The responsibility principle in this study appears to be supported by a large section of the Swedish population. As the economy becomes more organized and people less dependent on market forces, I would expect, according to Miller's theory, that an hierarchical view of distributive justice would become dominant. The results from this study suggests that Miller may be right. It also seems as if workers are more divided in their opinions as to what principles should be used in wage bargaining. White-collar workers are more consistently in favor of a single principle, the responsibility principle.

In wage negotiations there are mainly two categories of values: those which build on a notion of desert and those which build on a notion of equality. There may be a conflict between values based on these two notions.

Norms of distributive justice based on the notion of desert may emanate from an argument based on equality: in an exchange situation there should be a reasonable reciprocity or balance between the parties and when benefits and deprivations are distributed, equals should be treated as equals, at least in similar situations.[284]

We find already in this formulation the possibility of treating un-equals unequally. There is a measure of proportionality in concepts of distributive justice based on the notion of desert. Proportionality refers to the rule that the reward, or the benefit to be distributed, is to be divided between persons proportionally to the contribution they have made to the common good. The idea of proportionality can be found already in the writings of Aristotle who distinguished between "arithmetic" and "geometric" justice.

According to Aspelin (1977), Aristotle considered justice as a proper weighting of interests according to the principle of equality. The price of a product should reflect its value; the wage should reflect the amount of work done. But Aristotle distinguished between two kinds of equality: 1) Two workers perform equally well and thus can claim equal wages, two criminals commit the same crime and should therefore have the same punishment. In this case the principle "an equal for an equal" is valid and is called in Aristotle's words "arithmetic justice". 2) one person's contribution is more valuable than the other's. In this case he is entitled to a larger wage. A person commits a more offensive crime and should therefore get a more severe punishment. Here the principle of "geometric justice" is at work, and demands proportionality between an action and its consequences.[285]

The proportionality of the Aristotelian geometric justice distinguish it from equality as such. Andersson (1969) distinguishes similarly between ideologies of distributive justice based on inclusive and exclusive ideologies. Exclusive criteria are according to Andersson those which are based on the value of the work performance for production. Because different persons will perform differently according to such criteria, they are used to differentiate between persons and are thus exclusive. Inclusive criteria are those which apply to many or all in society. These deal with the minimum allowances of socially defined goods which everybody has a right to on the basis of being a member of the society and a participant in the labor market.[286] This distinction is also made in LO's wage political document from 1987.[287] Equality as a leading principle is contrasted with justice and it is acknowledged that they measure different things.

A resort to principles of justice in wage negotiation situations may reflect a wish to raise the level of discussions to a higher impartial level. To be just implies applying principles which are above egoistic behavior. Using principles of justice is a way to link one's own bargaining situation to common values, values shared not only within one's own group, but with a larger section of society. Still, the concepts of justice are seldom used to attack social and economic inequalities, on the contrary, the resort to principles of justice can explicitly endorse existing inequalities.[288]

When the existing hierarchy is legitimized with principles of distributive justice, these principles are used for a conservative purpose. The legitimization of hierarchy is also a legitimization of power. A concept such as responsibility can be used to legitimate hierarchies, and may thus serve conservative purposes.

It is clearly possible for professional groups to raise their status and to guard their position through the use of organizational power, monopoly and political influence. Afterward suitable principles of distributive justice can be applied in order to legitimate their new status.

It has been argued in this chapter that there exist differences between the wage policies of the unions in the Swedish WNS, differences which also can be found among the members of the organizations. I have argued that the principles of distributive justice which are chosen reflect the development of the economy and the work places. The competition between the unions is also evident in the differences in wage policies.

# Conclusions

In this book I have described the most recent developments in the Swedish wage negotiation system. However, this is more than a study of Sweden, it is also an application of Social rule systems theory in a concrete institutional setting. First, the structural formation and reformation of the Swedish wage bargaining system, particularly 'The Swedish Model' of centralized wage negotiation and administration, has been studied. The theoretical-methodological focus has been on identifying several key organizing rules which give the system its identifying properties.

A centralized wage bargaining system presupposes the existence of a norm which allows the central actors to determine the increases of wages. This is also a study of how such rules are broken against. It is argued that the wage drift of blue-collar workers not only depends on the supply and demand for labor, but also on labor bargaining power. It is shown how the actors in the system trie to compensate themselves through the invention of new rules: wage development guarantees.

Finally, I have presented an empirical study of distributive rules or conceptions of distributive justice. The support for the different principles among the members of different unions has been investigated.

In studying the "Swedish Model", I have examined factors which de-stabilize the system and set the stage for transition to other systems. I have suggested how the time frame can be periodized since the Second World War on the basis of characteristic organizing rules prevailing in each period.

In the post-war period four major negotiation regimes were identified. Different analytical models can be associated with the four epochs, where each epoch is expected to exhibit differing patterns of negotiation and conflict, negotiated outcomes, and wage performance.

In the first epoch (I), the organizing principle of the WNS was decentralized, that is branch specific, union-level negotiations for blue-collar workers. This system was transformed into a system with centralized LO-SAF negotiations, which characterized the second epoch (II). In the transition from epoch II to III, the centralized system with LO-SAF hegemony was transformed into a bi-polar system (III) with centralized private and public negotiations. A dominant game in this period entailed competition between public and private employee collectives, played out through their negotiations with representatives of public and private employers, respectively. At the end of epoch III, the wage negotiation system was transformed further into a multi-polar system (IV), involving complicated income distribution struggles between public and private, blue- and white-collar collectives. While in epoch II LO and SAF could disregard - or settle more on their own terms with - other groups of employees, in the later epochs other collectives had the power to insist on their terms. One major consequence of this development was to make the WNS much more complicated and difficult to stabilize or to maintain in stable states.

The Swedish Model was sustained over a long period (until the 1970s), because two powerful and important agents, SAF and LO as well as key political actors had an interest in maintaining it.

In changed contemporary circumstances, the SAF-LO coalition no longer dominates incomes policy, wage negotiations and wage developments as they had done earlier. New actors with diverse interests and aims have entered in the collective bargaining system. The wage formation process has developed into a wage-carousel where the demands of one labor union pushed up the demands of others. None of the actors enjoyed sufficient control over the situation to be able either to fulfill its goals or to establish a new system. This situation led to high uncertainty and increasing conflict potential.

The "Swedish Model" has not been able to totally control wage developments. Deviance in the form of wage drift has always been of concern in the centralized negotiations. Before 1966, SAF and LO negotiated exceptions from the central agreement in advance of the regular negotiations. After a while these negotiations expanded and the central negotiators became occupied with solving minuscule problems which really belonged to quite a different level. Eventually a technique was developed: the "Wage development guarantee". Such a guarantee compensates groups which have not experienced wage drift comparable to a calculated average.[289]

At first the wage development guarantee was a technique used only internally in the LO-SAF negotiations. Later, PTK elaborated a guarantee that compensated for blue-collar workers' wage drift, their guarantees and for wage drift for PTK's unions as well. In the public segment similar guarantees were developed. The effect was to lock the relative wage structure between the organizations. It was difficult for the LO collective to raise their wages more than other groups. The guarantees were one symptom of the changed focus of the system. Instead of a struggle between labor and capital over the distribution of the surplus between profits and wages, the struggle is now between the different unions in the different segments of the economy. While the use of wage development guarantees is opposed by the employers, this does not mean that the pressure for equal treatment from the unions side has abided.

Wage drift offers a possibility for smaller groups within the collectives to push ahead in earnings. Under piece-wages, the individual workers have the power to decide their own wages to a higher degree than under time-wages. Wage drift is thus a tool for some groups of workers in the struggle over the distribution of resources in Sweden.

Workers' wage drift has usually been explained with variables from the labor market such as unemployment or different measures of vacancies. Labor market explanations may leave the social processes which lead to wage drift as a "black box".

I have tried to argue that the labor market model does not fully explain wage drift phenomena. Wage drift can in large part be explained with other variables which focus our attention on the plant level, to processes and structures which feed wage drift. First, actual hiring practices seem not to be only dependent on wages as an incentive to recruit labor. Second, the increasing importance of the administrative management of personnel focuses on internal recruitment rather than on external recruitment. Instead the labor market seems to function as a norm to which employers and workers gear their ambitions.

Wage drift is a phenomena which can occur whenever less strict wage systems are used. When bargaining power conditions favor workers, employers with loose wage systems may find it hard to limit wage drift. A rising business cycle shifts the balance of power toward the workers. Wage drift may originally occur on piece-wages, but is rapidly spread through reference networks to time-wages and other more stable wage forms.

Companies have operational guidelines which lead them to follow the development of wages. They react to the information that is passed on through the reference networks. Unions also have reference networks and may in local bargains, force a development of wages which parallels that of other companies in the area or in the industry.

My conclusion is that workers can use their bargaining power to increase wage drift if conditions are favorable and they are given the opportunity. In this process piece-wages are especially important.

Principles of distributive justice play an important role in motivating and legitimizing claims and counter-claims relating to wages, and in negotiation processes. Such principles are formulated in the wage-policies of unions and are used in wage negotiations at all levels of the wage bargaining system. At the central level, comparisons between different unions play an important role in the negotiation process. At the local level, comparisons are often made between companies.

The most striking result of the investigation was the strong support for the "responsibility principle", 38% of the respondents said that this was the most proper principle. Even though the support was stronger among white-collar workers, it was the most widely supported principle among LO-members as well.

It seems as if LO-workers are more divided in their opinions of what principles should be used in wage bargaining. White-collar workers are more consistently in favor of a single principle, the responsibility principle.

As I have shown, the opinions of the members of each organization tend to be reflected in the organization's wage policy. LO is the organization with the most "radical" members, but it is also the organization which has the widest spectrum of opinions among its members.

The "responsibility" principle in this study is supported by a large proportion of the Swedish population. As the economy becomes more organized and people less dependent on market forces, I would expect that a hierarchical view of distributive justice will become dominant. The results from this study suggests that Miller may be right.

A resort to principles of justice in wage negotiation situations may reflect a wish to raise the level of discussions to a higher impartial level. To be just implies applying principles which are above egoistic behavior. Using principles of justice is a way to link one's own bargaining situation to common values, values shared not only within one's own group, but by a larger section of society. Still, the concepts of justice are seldom used to attack social and economic inequalities, on the contrary, the resort to principles of justice can explicitly endorse existing inequalities.[290]

When the existing hierarchy is legitimized with principles of distributive justice, these principles are used for a conservative purpose. The legitimization of hierarchy is also a legitimization of power. A concept such as responsibility can be used to legitimate hierarchies, and may thus serve conservative purposes.

It is clearly possible for professional groups to raise their status and to guard their position through the use of organizational power, monopoly and political influence. Afterward suitable principles of distributive justice can be applied in order to legitimate their new status.

Collective bargaining is more than a rule-governed exchange between two parties, be it in economic or other terms. The collective agreement is meant to ensure that whenever a transaction takes place in the labor market, it will take place according to the provisions of the agreement. These provisions are a set of rules intended to regulate the terms of employment contracts. Collective bargaining is thus in its *essence a rule-making process*. The effect of the negotiation of collective agreements is to impose certain limits on the freedom of the actors.[291]

On the basis of the power resources at their disposal, mobilized and utilized within an established rule-regime, the actors join in negotiations to shape and invent new rules. The rules are jointly determined by representatives of employers and employees who share responsibility for their contents and observance, often with legal underpinnings. Collective bargaining is thus analyzable not only in terms of its economic consequences, but also as a process of *'private politics', a rule-making process which resides outside parliament*. It follows that a union may be as interested in establishing its rights and action capabilities vis a vis employers as in achieving immediate material gains, such as wage increases.

Institutions, even the most successful ones must change, because the world around them changes. They also change because the social actors engaged in them, and their power relationships, change. The actors learn and develop new goals and strategies and, as a result, place new demands on the institutions. In this context, it is essential to see institutions as human devices, social rule systems, which enable diverse actors - even agents with somewhat different perspectives and interests - to coordinate their decisions and actions, to solve common problems and to resolve social conflicts in relatively effective ways.

The Swedish collective bargaining system was designed to reduce and to regulate conflicts between employers' and employees' organizations. It was never designed to deal - and the experience of the past 20 years has shown it incapable of dealing - with serious conflicts among labor groups and their organizations, in particular between white-collar and blue-collar unions, as well as between collectives in the private segment as opposed to those in the public segment. The WNS is segmented, with disorganized or uncoordinated but inter-linked, indirect negotiations. This has contributed to the 'wage carousel', with leapfrogging and instability as various labor unions and collectives struggle to stay ahead or to catch up with one another.

The current complex of problems are institutional in character. One may speak of a *mismatch* between the institutional set-up and the typical problems and conflicts to be handled. Such mismatches give rise to innovations and attempts to restructure the set-up. Often, such restructuring leads to serious group conflicts, in part about the types of innovation required to shape a genuinely new and effective system. At the present time in Sweden there is a stalemate around the maintenance/transformation of the system. On the one hand, the established Swedish model is unable to deal effectively with a set of new and difficult problems. On the other, key actors such as the state, VF, LO, SAF, etc. are unable either to impose their respective proposals for a solution or to agree to common organizing principles which could serve as a legitimizing point of departure for the establishment of a new system. In part, this is because of the absence of a dominant actor or coalition to establish and develop a new system, with new understandings and new principles and rules. Key actors and groups on the scene (e.g. VF, major export companies, Metall, LO, white-collar unions on the private side, those on the public side, and the state) have very different ideas about how a new system should be organized, for instance, to what extent it should be centralized (and, in a certain sense, a continuation of the present system); or what relationships should obtain between the private and public segments; and what principles - or more precisely, what ranking of principles - of distributive justice should prevail in income determination

In my view, then, one of the major shortcomings, if not the major one, of the Swedish Model is its incapability of regulating - or resolving - destabilizing conflicts among labor unions and struggles between public and private segments over income distribution.

The present measures toward decentralization may lead to the erosion of solidarity norms, which in turn may lead to a fiercer competition between local groups over wages.

The segmented collective bargaining system with powerful independent unions making relative comparisons and struggling with one another - often indirectly through negotiations with employers - generates a difficult and in a certain sense unpredictable, wage negotiation process. From the perspective of many employers and employees in the export and open sectors of the economy, the system is ineffective and, indeed, entails considerable risks. If the outcomes of wage negotiation games are not predictable, a realistic planning of labor cost developments and investment decisions becomes unfeasible. Thus, one important motivation in sustaining the system weakens or disappears, thereby eroding commitment or loyalty to the system among some major actors. Moreover, there are powerful tendencies in the system to generate wage agreements which ignore some of the pressing demands and constraints of international markets and export branches.

This book has suggested the usefulness of sociological concepts in the analysis of industrial relations and for the understanding of the contemporary problems facing the Swedish wage negotiation system. Conflict and struggle, to varying degrees, are endemic to capitalist societies. Institutions have been developed to structure and regulate conflicts between capital and labor. It is more difficult to create institutions that regulate conflicts between different worker collectives.

It has been shown that the competition between different segments has contributed to the present difficulties in the WNS. To some degree, the difficulties have to do with how to handle the fact that wages drift, that there is no total control over wage developments. Also, the members of the different collectives have different opinions of how wages are to be distributed. This book offers no solutions, but it points out new areas which have to be systematically investigated.

# Appendix: Organizations in the Swedish Wage Negotiation System.

**LO**: "Landsorganisationen" is an association of 24 unions organizing blue-collar workers. The largest union is **SKAF** (the municipal workers' union) with 617,498 members (1984) followed by **Metall,** (the metal workers' union) with 450,293 members. LO is the largest association of workers in the labor market and has totally 2,238,588 members. The member unions have both regional offices ("avdelningar" and "sektioner") and plant level shops ("klubbar").

**PTK**: "Privattjänstemannakartellen" is an association of white-collar workers' unions in the private sector of the economy. PTK negotiates for TCO-unions as well as SACO/SR-unions. **SIF**, ("Svenska Industritjänstemannaförbundet") is the largest TCO-union within PTK with 274,257 members. **CF**, ("Civilingenjörsförbundet") is the largest SACO/SR-union within PTK and has 34,870 members. **SALF** is the foremen's union.

**SAC:** The syndicalist union. It organizes workers at all different levels and sectors. It had in 1980 18,221 members.

**SAF**: "Svenska Arbetsgivarföreningen" is the Swedish employers' organization in the private sector and negotiates with LO and PTK. SAF organizes 37 employers' organizations with 38,426 companies who are members and owners of SAF. The largest association is **VF**, ("Verkstadsföreningen") which has 2,256 member companies who employ 318.737 employees.

**SFO:** SFO is the employers' organization for companies owned by the state. SFO was established in 1970 when the state decided to organize its companies outside of SAF.

**KFO:** KFO is the negotiating organization for the companies belonging to the cooperative movement.

**TA:** TA is the employers' organization for newspapers. Newspapers are in a special position because of their reporting and opinion forming function.

They have therefore chosen to organize themselves in a separate organization.

**KAB**: KAB is the employers' organization for public housing projects.

# The State Sector

There are a number of organizations in the state sector.

**SF**: SF is the union organizing workers in the state sector. SF is a member of LO and has 202,801 members.

**TCO-S**: TCO-S is a section of TCO which negotiates for TCO unions in the state sector. The largest member union is ST (Statstjänstemannaförbundet)

**SACO/SR-S**: SACO/SR-S is a section of SACO/SR which negotiates for state employees.

**SAV**: "Statens arbetsgivarverk" is the employers' organization in the state sector. SAV was created in 1965 when the white-collar workers in the state sector got their lawful right to strike. SAV is governed by the X-department and the secretary of the X-department is the chairman of its board. SAV has difficulties acting on its own and has to coordinate its efforts with the department of Finance.

# The Municipal sector

**SKAF**: "Svenska Kommunalarbetarförbundet" is LO's largest member union. SKAF negotiates for the workers employed by the municipal sector.

**KTK**: "Kommunaltjänstemannakartellen" represents TCO-unions with members working for local or county municipalities. SKTF ("Svenska Kommunaltjänstemannaförbundet") is the largest member organization.

**SACO/SR-K**: SACO/SR-K is the municipal negotiation organization for SACO/SR unions.

**Svenska Kommunförbundet**: "Svenska Kommunförbundet" is a peak organization coordinating the local municipalities, it is also their bargaining organization.

**Landstingsförbundet**: "Landstingsförbundet" is a peak organization for counties. It negotiates in wage matters with the unions in the municipal sector.

# Footnotes

1     Research on the wage negotiation and formation process has been relatively limited in Sweden. Hart and von Otter (1973) wrote a book on the local wage formation process. Among Swedish political scientists there is a tradition of research in the fields of union democracy, the development of unions and corporatism. Elvander (1969) has written about interest organizations in Sweden. In a more recent study, Elvander (1988) depicted in detail the wage negotiations in the crucial years 1982-1986.[1] A recent study of SAF's history of negotiations 1930 to 1970 has been written by DeGeer (1986). Earlier studies also include Norgren (1941) and Johnston (1963) who wrote about the early Swedish collective bargaining system. Martin's (1984) study of the peculiarities of the Swedish model has been a very valuable source. The economists Hansen and Rehn (1956), Schager (1981, 1987, 1988), and Nilsson (1987) have all contributed to the discussion about wage drift.

       It would seem natural for sociologists to study the interaction, power play, and manipulation occurring in negotiations in a systematic way, but efforts in this direction have been few. The nearest sociology comes to a theory of negotiations is probably found in Strauss's (1978) conceptualization of a negotiated order and negotiation processes, or in the works of Walton and McKersie (1965). Social-psychologist, such as Bacharach and Lawler have started to look into the phenomena of negotiations and tactics.

       Among political scientists there have been some attempts to analyze negotiations. Schelling (1960) has written one important book, "The Strategy of Conflict". There is a research tradition in the USA in the field of collective wage-bargaining. One significant theoretical work is Stevens' (1963) "Strategy and Collective Bargaining Negotiations".

       Swedish wage negotiations have been the subject of some studies such as Hart and Otter's (1973) book on local wage determination, Victorin's (1973) legalistic study of the Swedish wage and salary system, and the earlier mentioned study by Elvander (1988). While Nilsson (1985) wrote an excellent study of white-collar unions in Sweden, he fails to see the tension between these and blue-collar unions which is evident in the study of collective bargaining.

       Korpi (1978) (1983) is a proponent of the Marxist study of industrial relations. In *The Working Class under Welfare Capitalism* he traces the development of the power bases of capitalism and organized labor in Sweden and tries to assess whether labor can function as the antithesis of capital.

2     Dunlop 1958, pp. 7-13.

3     Dunlop 1958, pp. 13-14.

4     Roche 1986, p. 7.

5     Flanders 1969, p. 14.

6     Flanders 1969, p. 14.

7     Flanders 1969, p. 19.

8     Burns and Flam 1987, p. 8. see also Giddens 1984.

9     Burns and Flam 1987, p. 9.

10    The following section builds largely on Burns et al Man, Decision, and Society (Burns et al 1985)

11    Baumgartner et al 1976.

12    Burns et al 1985.

13    Burns et al 1985.

14    Burns and Flam 1987, p. 8.

15    Ashby 1964, pp. 206-208.

16    Korpi 1974.

17    Thibaut and Kelley draw upon 'game theory' in developing their framework. But they wisely avoid some of the unrealistic assumptions and non-sociological features of game-theory. Game-theorists try to determine how a rational actor who is trying to maximize his gain chooses strategically between different alternatives of behavior. The actor has to take into consideration the choices of the opposite party. Game theorists want to show how the actor chooses the optimal strategy. (Bacharach and Lawler 1981, p. 7.)

One of the most important assumptions of game-theory, according to Bacharach and Lawler, is that parties will accept a common definition of the situation. This is quite an unrealistic assumption which emphasizes the drawbacks of game theory. Game-theory is weak on the following accounts, according to Bacharach and Lawler:

1    *Realism*. Actual bargaining does not allow for those assumptions which are necessary for game-theory.

2    *Application*. The lack of realism makes it almost impossible to test the models empirically.

3    *Informativeness*. The search for a determinate solution causes a loss of informativeness. All that Nash and Raiffa can tell us is that the midpoint is a likely solution.

4    *They neglect the bargaining process*. Tactical and manipulative action becomes a disturbance in their theories.

5    *The environment is neglected*. It is assumed that the effect of the environment upon the bargaining process acts through the utility function of the actors.(Bacharach and Lawler 1981, p. 15-16.)

18    Thibaut and Kelley (1959) present a social psychological theory which is suited for game-theoretical analysis. Their starting point is that the essence of any interpersonal relationship is interaction. Each person is equipped with a repertoire of behavior directed to the attainment of a goal. This is called a behavior sequence or behavior set. The outcomes of interaction are stated in terms of rewards and costs. This enables the authors to create a matrix of possible interactions and outcomes. The matrix describes a non-zero-sum game with no fixed values. (Thibaut and Kelley 1959, pp. 10-13.)

19    Walton and McKersie (1965) distinguish between two main approaches to the study of negotiations. Negotiations can be said to entail integrative and distributive bargaining. Distributive bargaining refers to the process in which one party tries to obtain his goals when these goals are in conflict with the other party's goal. In game-theoretical terms it is called a fixed sum game. Integrative bargaining refers to the case where both parties have goals which are not in fundamental conflict with each other. The corresponding game-theoretical term is a variable-sum game. Walton and McKersie also study two more aspects of negotiations: attitudinal structuring and intra-organizational bargaining.

20    Ross 1948.

21    Burns et al 1984.

22    Korpi 1983, p. 16.

23 In the strike in the pulp-mills in 1932 the employers had joined an international cartel in which they had to reduce production by 30 %. The strike's consequence was that the employers fulfilled the demands from the cartel. (Casparsson 1948)

24 Giddens 1984; Burns et al 1985; Burns and Flam 1987.

25 Burns and Flam 1987.

26 An earlier version of this chapter was published in Burns and Flam (1987).

27 DeVille and Burns, 1977.

28 See Flanders 1969, especially pp.14-16.

29 The peak organizations are LO, TCO, SAF etc. They are associations of organizations and the main actors in the central arena.

30 In Swedish: arbetare and tjänstemän.

31 See Appendix.

32 A kitty is a clause in the agreement that stipulates that part of the wage increase is to be handed out in a predetermined way. There have existed kitties for women, low-income earners etc.

33 Ullenhag, 1971.

34 Ullenhag, 1971.

35 This, as later 'historic compromises' between capital and a significant but not all-inclusive labor movement, must be viewed in the context of more radical as well as anarchistic movements among workers. The latter were perceived as more threatening and unacceptable to employers - and political authorities - than mainline, largely social democratic unions.

36 Martin 1984, p. 196.

37 Korpi 1983 p. 45.

38 Westerståhl 1945, pp. 146,154.

39 ibid.

40 Nordin 1981, p. 207.

41 Meidner 1973, p. 28-32.

42 ibid. p. 32-33.

43 ibid. p. 35

44 ibid. pp. 35-36.

45 ibid. p. 35.

46 Burns and Olsson, 1986; Lash, 1984.

47 Such increases, not authorized by the central LO/SAF agreement, are referred to as wage-drift and are 'negotiated' at branch, enterprise or plant levels. See further chapter 4.

48 Burns and Olsson, 1986.

49 OECD National Accounts, Main Economic Indicators and Economic Outlook.

50 Martin 1984, pp. 239-240.

51 From an interview with K-O Faxén.

52 SAF 1982.

53 SAF took the initiative in 1967 to propose a new, highly structured procedure for simultaneously negotiating wages for both blue and white collar workers. The committee got its name from the research directors of TCO, SAF, and LO: Gösta Edgren, Karl-Olof Faxén and Claes-Erik Odhner, who were to produce the EFO-report.

The model was build around the ramifications of the two-sector model of inflation in a small open economy presented by the Norwegian economist Odd Aukrust.

The economy is divided into two sectors: the competitive or C sector and the sheltered or S sector. The C sector is open to international competition while the outputs of the S sector is neither export nor subject to competition from imports. In the C-sector, prices are set on the world market, while in the S-sector, mark-up pricing is normal. Exchange rates are assumed to be fixed and the productivity growth is higher in the C-sector than in the S-sector. Wage growth is the same in both sectors, the C-sector being the wage leader. Wage increases are transmitted through the solidaristic wage policy.

Since productivity growth is lower in the S-sector, profit margins can only be maintained in that sector through raising prices more than in the C-sector. This makes the domestic inflation rate higher than the rate of price increases on the world market. What is important for a small country like Sweden is not so much inflation as the continued competitiveness of the C-sector. An essential condition is that a sufficient level of investment can be maintained.

The relationship between wages, prices and profits are analyzed in terms of the 'margin' or 'room' for increases from the growth of the C-sector. This margin correspond to the sum of international price increases and the increased C-sector productivity. The distribution of this margin between profits and wages is determined in collective bargaining. (Martin 1984, p. 243)(Edgren et al. 1970)

54    Martin 1984, p. 247.

55    Martin 1984, pp. 265-268.

56    Interview with Karl-Olof Faxén 1983-11-02.

57    Martin 1984, p. 292.

58    SAF: Fakta om Sveriges Ekonomi, 1986.

59    ibid.

60    Sweden's economic performance was generally weak during the 1970s and early 1980s (Turner, 1985) Economic growth and industrial production lagged, the latter even declining during the latter part of the 1970s (Turner, 1985) Swedish export industry suffered a sharp decline in international competitiveness, under the generally prevailing conditions of recession. Falling market shares cut export revenues at the same time that government subsidies, other transfer payments and budget deficits supported indirectly an increased import bill. The result was chronic deficits in external accounts. (Turner, 1985)

61    There are various explanations of the conflict. (see Broström, 1981), which we shall not explore here. One factor was the tactical maneuvering of the peak labor market actors in the private and public segment vis a vis one another. This complex interplay between public and private segments, without the benefit of a framework for negotiation or even deliberation -- certainly increased the likelihood of misunderstanding and miscalculation.

62    Analyses of the type presented in this section have been developed independently by Suarez and Goldborne (1986); also see Baumgartner et al. (1986), Burns (1987)

63    This is not meant to imply that economic and political forces play no role in the establishment or transformation of a regime or in its stability. Indeed, the analyses of this chapter point out some of these linkages.

64    For instance, in the agreement for 1966, LO introduced a wage development guarantee. The aim was to ensure that groups which did not benefit from wage drift could maintain their levels without the procedure of negotiations-about-exceptions which earlier had been customary. This was in a sense a foreboding of times to come. The struggle over differentials took the form of attempts to establish -- or prevent the establishment of -- wage development guarantees. The battle of differentials was well on its way.

65    The sources of our data are indicated below:

*Worker's wages*: The statistics come from different sources. The period 1946-1960 comes from Johnston (1962) and refers to adult men. The period 1961-1963 comes from Martin (1984), and the period 1964-1983 has been provided by SAF (1983), both periods refers to all blue-collar workers. The data refers to the private sector.

*White-collar workers wages*: The statistics have been provided by SAF (1982b). The total can be presented in two ways: first as a raw sum, secondly as a measure standardized for among other variables: age. The data refers to the private sector of the economy.

*Economic indicators*: Here we present only a few economic indicators: change in GNP, the period 1960-1983 comes from SAF (1983), the earlier period from SCB (1957) and SCB (1962); inflation measured as CPI comes from SAF (1983) and the period before 1960 from SCB (1969); unemployment (as percent of labor force comes from SCB (1954, 1956, 1963, 1975, and 1984b) The period before 1962 is measured as % of union members while therafter the measure is % of the labor force; public employment comes from SCB (1974); industry profits (as percent of turnover from SAF (1983); change in productivity comes from SAF(1983); change in industrial production comes from SAF (1983) and the period before 1960 from SCB (1955, 1958, 1962); state's balance (as percent of GNP comes from SCB (1984); increases in employment taxes or fees comes from SAF (1984); working days lost in industrial conflicts comes from "Förlikningsmannaexpeditionen" and SCB (1962); 'wild-cat' strikes (working days lost in industrial conflicts), from "Förlikningsmannaexpeditionen"; white-collar degree of organization (Kjellberg, 1983); relative size LO/TCO (Kjellberg 1983)

66     I am again struggling with the problem of being an outsider in the bargaining process. This has forced me to use secondary material for the description of the wage rounds. The sources have been material from the organizations, such as chronologies of the wage-rounds, for some organizations we have had access to some protocols. For the period 1984 to 1986, I have not conducted any field work of my own, but relied on the detailed study of Elvander (1988). The written material has been complemented with interviews with persons within the organizations. Instead of interviewing the chairmen and head-negotiators, we have targeted the level below, those with responsibility for the analytical (utredning) departments at the organizations. I am especially grateful of the support from Karl-Olof Faxén previously at SAF and Ingvar Ohlsson at LO.

67     Broström ed. 1981, pp 30-46.

68     ibid.

69     ibid.

70     ibid.

71     ibid.

72     ibid.

73     ibid.

74     Broström ed. 1981, p 147

75     Broström ed. 1981, p 74.

76     Broström ed. 1981, p 57.

77     Broström ed. 1981, p 148.

78     An increase in wages to be divided locally.

79     Internal SAF-document 1980-09-03: a memo for a speech held by Olof Ljunggren.

80     Edgren et al., 1970.

81     In Swedish: "Representantskap".

82     LO-Nytt no 7, February 4 1981.

83     ibid.

84     SAF, Annual Account 1981, p. 23.

85     SAF: Letter to the managing directors in SAF's member associations, 1981-03-06.

86     SAF, Annual Account 1981, p. 24-26.

87     SAF, Statutes 1982-06-29, p 25. If it is in ones power to perform certain actions, it is possible to be coerced into doing it. If one does not want to be forced to perform these actions, it is wise to see to it that they remain outside of one's area of decision, or authority. The contradictory nature of SAF's statutes may be used as an instrument to avoid getting caught in a conflict over the form of negotiations.

88     LO: Bakgrund och Fakta, Avtalsrörelsen 1983, pp. 4-6.

89     ibid. p 8. The dispute was about how much blue-collar workers' wage drift had actually been. The wage drift was decided to be just a trifle below the point where the wage development guarantee could be applied.

90    ibid. p. 9.
91    ibid. pp. 12-15.
92    ibid. pp. 17-18.
93    Interview with Ingvar Ohlsson LO 1983, Göte Larsson Metall 1983.
94    Interview with Ingvar Ohlsson LO 1983.
95    LO: Bakgrund och Fakta, Avtalsrörelsen 1983, pp. 20-21.
96    TCO-S Statstjänstemännens löneförhandlingar 1983.
97    Speech by Bertil Blomqvist at SIF general council 1983-05-17.
98    ibid.
99    SIF, general council 1983-09-07.
100    Elvander 1988, p. 139
101    ibid., p. 141-142.
102    ibid., p. 144.
103    ibid., p. 147.
104    ibid., p. 148.
105    ibid., p. 152-154.
106    ibid., p. 159.
107    ibid., p. 163-171.
108    ibid., p. 173.
109    ibid., p. 180.
110    ibid., p. 182-184.
111    ibid., p. 189-197.
112    ibid., p. 206.
113    ibid., p. 215-230.
114    ibid., p. 231-247.
115    ibid.
116    SAF Promemoria 82-05-04.
117    SAF Promemoria 82-05-04.
118    Interview with Karl-Olof Faxén.
119    These guarantees are actually called "förtjänstutvecklingsgaranti" or "FUG" which could be translated as "earnings development gurantee".
120    In Swedish the term is "egentlig industri".
121    SAF 1982.
122    ibid. (In Swedish the term is "avtalsområde").
123    ibid.
124    ibid.
125    ibid.
126    ibid.
127    ibid.
128    ibid.
129    ibid.
130    ibid.
131    ibid.
132    ibid.

133  The cooperation between the unions in the public segment was given this nick-name. The unions are: SF, SKAF, TCO-S and TCO

134  Broström 1981.

135  Wage-drift became a part of the central agreements between SAF and LO through the introduction of wage-development guarantees introduced in 1966. In this agreement wage-drift was defined as the difference between the statistically calculated development of time-wages and the estimated implications of the agreement. Time-wages are not adjusted for changes in the composition of wage forms, work-force or companies within the industry. The implications of the agreement are measured as the calculated immediate effect of industry level agreements. These are estimated by the employers organizations. The figures are thereafter collected and aggregated into figures for the whole SAF/LO jurisdiction and for manufacturing industry. Low-wage supplements and other agreed upon components are all included in the calculated effects of the agreement. Local increases above the industry level agreement are not included, but are defined as wage drift. (*Löneglidningen inom SAF/LO-området*, SAF/LOs gemensamma statistiknämnd, Stockholm 1982 pp 3-4.)

Wage drift can be registered when companies with low wages close down and when structural changes result in diminishing the number of low-paid jobs and increasing the number of well-paid jobs within the unit of calculation. That is, wage drift may be partly an effect of structural changes within a company or an industry which do not actually result in increased wages.

136  Interview with Karl-Olof Faxén.

137  Olsson 1989.

138  For a discussion of LO's wage policy see Chapter five.

139  SAF 1986.

140  TCO: Lönepolitikens samhällsekonomiska förutsättningar, 1982, pp. 11,31.

141  See Hansen and Rehn (1956), Jacobsson and Lindbäck (1969) (1971) and Schager 1988

142  Schager 1987.

143  Hansen and Rehn 1956.

144  Hansen and Rehn 1956, pp. 89-91.

145  Hansen and Rehn 1956, pp. 112,133.

146  Schager 1981.

147  Schager 1988.

148  Schager 1988.

149  Holmlund and Skedinger 1988, p. 2.

150  Holmlund and Skedinger 1988, p. 7.

151  Nilsson 1987, p. 19.

152  Reynolds 1951, p. 159.

153  By "close companies", Reynolds means companies which are close geographically and have similar production processes. See Reynolds 1951, p. 159.

154  Nilsson 1987, pp. 21-22.

155  Dahlström 1969, p. 22.

156  Eskilsson 1966, pp. 56-57.

157  Dahlström 1969, p. 16.

158  Dahlström 1969, p. 17.

159  Reynolds 1951, p. 201.

160  Eskilsson 1966, p. 59.

161  Eskilsson 1966, p. 59.

162    Eskilsson 1966, p. 60.

163    Olsson 1986.

164    Eskilsson 1966 p. 61.

165    See appendix.

166    Eskilsson 1966.

167    LO 1981, pp. 80-83.

168    Schager 1982.

169    See chapter two.

170    Economic theory seems to think that the only option for workers is "exit" (See Hirschman 1970). The fact that there are unions makes the "voice" option more fruitful. There appears to be a real possibility of expressing claims within the company. (See Freedman and Medoff 1984)

171    Holmlund 1984.

172    Only for mechanics did Schager get a correlation that was significantly different from zero, but only at the 7% level. Schager 1982, p. 254.

173    Schager 1982, p. 256.

174    Holmlund and Skedinger 1988, pp. 21-23.

175    Dahlström 1969, p. 22.

176    Brown et al (1984) found that the great majority of "overaward" payments in Australia take the form of a uniform payment to everyone of a given occupational grade within a given establishment (p 169.)

177    Olsson 1986.

178    ibid. p. 18.

179    Reynolds 1951, pp. 208-209.

180    Reynolds 1951, pp. 208-209.

181    Reynolds 1951, pp. 208-209.

182    Rundblad 1964.

183    Eskilsson 1966, p. 61.

184    Nilsson and Zetterberg 1987, pp. 10-16, 29.

185    Holmlund 1984, p. 187.

186    Holmlund 1984, p. 107. Reynolds found little evidence that a high wage level causes workers to apply at a particular plant, because most workers in his study knew very little about comparative wages in various plants. The advantage of a high wage is to persuade those who apply to accept employment with the company. If the wages are very low, most applicants will find that the rates offered them are below previous earnings, and they might reject the offer. If the wage level is high, most applicants will be ready to accept them.(Reynolds 1951, pp. 161-162)

187    Reynolds 1951, p. 215.

188    Åberg 1985, p. 22.

189    Åberg 1985, p. 23.

190    Åberg 1985, p. 23-24.

191    Åberg 1985, p. 38-39.

192    Åberg 1985, pp. 44-45.

193    Reynolds 1951, p. 161.

194    Hart and von Otter 1973, p. 127.

195    Finlay 1987, p. 50.

196    Finlay 1987, p. 65.

197    Finlay 1987, p. 65.

198   Olsson 1986,  p. 46.

199   By "excess" profits I mean a level of profits which is regarded socially as being too large.

200   Howard and Tolles, 1974, p. 548.

201   Howard and Tolles, 1974, p. 548.

202   Martin 1984, p. 292.

203   SAF 1986.

204   LO 1986, pp. 57-59.

205   See Mishel 1986; Howard and Tolles 1974; Navarro (1983); Long and Link 1983; Brown et al. 1984.

206   Mishel 1986, p. 90.

207   Mishel 1986, p. 102.

208   Mishel 1986, p. 102.

209   Howard and Tolles, 1974, p. 551.

210   Navarro 1983, p. 226.

211   Long and Link 1983, p. 249.

212   Blanchflower and Oswald 1988, p. 366-367.

213   The Insider-outsider theory of wages does not contradict my findings. Blanchflower and Oswald describes the theory: *"The key characteristic of these models is the stress they place upon firms internal activities and financial performance. Wages, in this framework, are determined at least in large part by how well the employers are doing. If sales boom, insiders' demand higher pay from their firms. 'Outsiders', such as the unemployed, have little or no role to play".* (Blanchflower and Oswald 1988, p. 364)

Oswald (1985) has shown that bargaining models also can generate similar predictions.

Solow (1985) has presented an insider-outsider model of wage determination. He tries to explain the persistence of unemployment over a wide range of fluctuations of aggregate demand with the willingness and ability of insiders to convert higher demand in to higher wages for themselves rather than into increased access to jobs for outsiders. (Solow 1985, p. 427)

Blanchflower and Oswald found no significant differences between union and non-union companies, except that merit/individual performance was an important factor in the non-union sector. (Blanchflower and Oswald 1988, p. 367-368)

214   Blanchflower and Oswald 1988, p. 367.

215   Brown et al 1984, pp. 171-172.

216   Brown et al 1984, p. 171.

217   As was earlier argued by Reynolds!

218   There is an example of bad labor timing from the Paper and Pulp conflict in Sweden in 1932. The slump in demand led the producers to initiate the formation of a production restricting cartel. The workers were at the same time faced with a cut in wages. As they choose to go on strike, production was decreased enough to keep up prices and the employers saved a considerable amount on wages which they did not have to pay. It was the strategy of LO to get control over such strike movements in order to save energy for periods when employers were more ready to give in to worker demands. (See Casparsson 1947)

219   The risk of unemployment is a possible measure of employee vulnerability. The Swedish case with even in hard times, in international terms a low level of unemployment, suggests that it can be justified to for the moment, direct the focus on other concepts.

220   Vulnerability is a concept similar to that of commitment as discussed by Bacharach and Lawler (1981). Commitment to them means a commitment to the issues at stake in the bargaining. Similarly vulnerability reflects the value of the outcome, if one party attaches a great value to an outcome, he becomes more vulnerable. (Bacharach and Lawler 1981, p.62)

221    The material for this part has been collected in two main ways: an abundant use has been made of secondary statistics, collected by SCB, SAF and other researchers. I have also interviewed union and employer representatives in 6 companies in the Uppsala region plus officials in a number of national unions and employers associations. A measure of the implementation of central agreements has been obtained from Schager.

There are a number of difficulties in using this kind of material:

The number of cases is small, the data on manufacturing consist of 15 cases. The small number of cases make it difficult to estimate all the variables.

Wage drift figures have been obtained from the Joint SAF-LO statistics and consist of a time series, for the whole of industry proper (Egentlig Industri, SNI3) SAF (1982). Measures for the business cycle have been obtained from SCB (TSDB), data which has been collected by Konjunkturinstiutet. These data consist of appraisals of the stock of orders, number of firms working at full capacity and appraisals of the stock of finished products. The profit measure used has been net profits for the whole of industry as presented by SAF (1983). A measure for the capital/labor measure in different branches has been obtained from SIND (. SIND measures the net profit share of value added. Wage drift arises to a large extent in the process of implementing centrally negotiated contracts. A measure of this effect has been elaborated by Schager (1988) and is used here. The variable measures the number of agreements implemented during the measuring period.

The timing of the variables seems to be of the utmost importance in the case of wage drift. Wage drift is calculated on a 2nd quarter to 2nd quarter basis, while much other data is collected on a yearly basis. First, the causal order assumed must be consistent with time. Second, the possibilities of lags must be taken into account. Lags are important when profits are analyzed. Profits are defined in the annual accounts of the companies. It can be assumed that past profits are more important for workers. Due to the way profit is measured, the present profit will not be known during the period when it occurs. Known profits are those of the year before. For profits we have only calender year data, here it shows that a lag of 1,5 years produces the best fit. A significant effect arises for a lag of 2,5 year, but the coefficient has the wrong sign.

The model is as follows:

| Variable | Parameter estimate | F | Prob F |
|----------|--------------------|-----|--------|
| Intercept | 2.47 | 2.9 | 0.010 |
| Profit$_{t-0.5}$ | 0.20 | 1.07 | 0.30 |
| Profit$_{t-1.5}$ | 0.65 | 2.53 | 0.02 |
| Profit$_{t-2.5}$ | -0.60 | -2.29 | 0.04 |
| Profit$_{t-3.5}$ | 0.27 | 1.41 | 0.18 |
| Model | $R^2 = 0.57$ | 5.0 | 0.009 |
| DF=4 | DW=1.978 | | |

222    From SIND 1980:2. The measure is an average for the period 1969-1977.

223 The figure is for SNI 351-352 excluding the rubber industry (included in SNI 3)

224 The implementation variable emanates from Schager 1988.

225 See for example the discussion in Hyman and Brough (1975).

226 Olsson 1986, pp. 13,14,23.

227 Olsson 1986, p. 39.

228 Interview notes.

229 According to internal SAF-reports.

230 Olsson 1986.

231 Ross 1948, p 53.

232 Ross 1948, pp 53-63.

233 Ross 1948, pp 53-57.

234 LO 1986.

235 Nilsson 1987.

236 The sources of the wage policies were the official documents from the actors themselves, such as congress reports and pamphlets. It can be argued that such documents are of little value in discovering "real" wage policies. This would have to be done through observing actual behavior in wage negotiations. (See for example Ross 1948) It has however been outside the scope of my research opportunities to follow the negotiations so closely. A valuable source on the wage policies of white-collar workers is Nilsson (1985).

237 The use of this SIFO data has been a mixed blessing. The data has a high quality, being based on interviews with a large sample and having a reasonable response rate. Financial and practical restrictions have however reduced the opportunities for analysis to a number of cross-tabulations. With more resources, a more extended statistical analysis of the data would have been possible.

238 Lockwood 1975, pp. 19-20.

239 Miller 1976, p. 22.

240 Miller 1976, p. 20.

241 Miller 1976, p. 21.

242 Miller 1976, pp. 148-149.

243 Scott 1987, Ross 1948

244 Kjellberg 1983, p. 276.

245 Other important organizations are the cartels, such as KTK, PTK, and TCO-S.

246 Nilsson 1985, p. 167.

247 LO 1951, pp. 133,136-.

248 Hadenius 1976, pp. 76-77.

249 LO 1971, p. 29.

250 Offe 1985.

251 Offe 1985, p. 183.

252 LO 1971.

253 LO 1981.

254 LO 1987.

255 LO 1987, pp. 11-12.

256 LO 1987, p. 13.

257 LO 1987, p. 24.

258 TCO 1963.

259 Nilsson 1985, p. 170 and Sandberg 1969, p. 114.

260 TCO 1982, p. 9.

261   Nilsson 1985, p. 170.

262   TCO 1973, pp. 132-134.

263   TCO 1982, p. 25.

264   TCO 1985, p. 21.

265   SIF 1976, p. 33.

266   SIF 1976, pp. 69-.

267   KTK 1979, p. 27 and TCO 1985, p. 39.

268   SACO/SR 1980, p. 103.

269   SACO/SR 1980, p. 99.

270   Nilsson 1985, p. 170-171

271   SAF 1979.

272   SAF 1979, p. 7.

273   SAF 1979, p. 3-.

274   The wording of the questions is of the utmost importance in this kind of analysis. The question asked was how the subjects would want to distribute a wage increase, the responses were phrased in a very general manner. The perhaps most general response was that which dealt with responsibility. This question is unfortunately open to many interpretations. The subjects were not offered a clear definition of responsibility, they only reacted to the word "responsibility" in the question. Responsibility can be interpreted in many ways: 1) responsibility over economic values, 2) responsibility over life and death, 3) responsibility as meaning a higher hierarchical level ( a boss). There may even be more ways to interpret the word. That it is an important issue is however supported by other studies such as Jaques (1956). In this study I have further elaborated one interpretation of "responsibility" in an attempt to understand the positive response to the question.

275   Whether "same percentage increase"-principle is a non-differentiating principle can be discussed. It can be argued that this principle differentiates according to the wage a person or a group has. While it is not necessarily an non-differentiating principle (since it gives more in absolute terms to those with higher incomes) it can be argued that it is rather a status-quo solution. If it is applied, this principle does not alter the different persons' or groups' share of the cake that is to be divided. LO has tried to move away from such principles, since they do not alter wage differential, while TCO on the other hand has been positive to such principles in actual negotiations.

276   SAF Annual Report 1982.

277   Hedström 1986, pp. 10-14.

278   Korpi and Åberg 1985, p. 24.

279   Ross 1948, p. 51.

280   Ross 1948, p. 51.

281   Miller 1976, pp. 301-304.

282   Miller 1976, pp. 83-.

283   Miller 1976, pp. 308-309.

284   Hyman and Brough 1975, p. 8.

285   Aspelin 1977, p. 132.

286   Andersson 1969, pp. 31-32.

287   LO 1987, p. 13.

288   Hyman and Brough 1975, p. 5.

289   Interview with Karl-Olof Faxén.

290   Hyman and Brough 1975, p. 5.

291   Flanders 1969, pp.14-16.

# Bibliography

Allen, V.L. *The Sociology of Industrial Relations: Studies in Method*. London: 1971.

Andersson Bo. "Några reflexioner om rättvisa och jämlikhet", von Otter Ed. *Arbetslivet i kris och förvandling*. Stockholm: Rabén & Sjögren 1974.

Ashby W. Ross. *An Introduction to Cybernetics*. London: Methuen & Co Ltd 1964.

Aspelin Gunnar. *Tankens vägar: en översikt av filosofins utveckling*. Lund: DOXA, 1981.

Bacharach, Samuel, B; Edward J. Lawler. *Power and Politics in Organizations*. San Francisco: Jossey-Bass Publishers, 1980.

Bacharach, Samuel, B; Edward J. Lawler. *Bargaining*. San Francisco: Jossey-Bass Publishers, 1981.

Baumgartner, Tom; Walter Buckley; Tom R. Burns; Peter Schuster. "Meta-Power and the Structuring of Social Hierarchies". Appears in T.R Burns & Walter Buckley (eds), *Power and Control*, London: Sage, 1976.

Baumgartner, Tom; Tom R. Burns; Philippe DeVille. *The Shaping of Socioeconomic Systems*. London/New York: Gordon and Breach, 1986.

Bengtsson Lars et al. *SAF och avtalsrörelserna 1980-1983 - det svenska förhandlingssytemet i förändring*. Stockholm: Stockholm University, Department of Political Science, 1984.

Bjermer Ulf et al. *Medling - två uppsatser om konfliktlösning på arbetsmarknaden*. Stockholm: Arbetslivscentrum, 1983.

Blackaby F.T. (ed) *The Future of Pay Bargaining*. London: 1980.

Blain A.N.J. and Gennard J. "Industrial Relations Theory: a Critical Review". *British Journal of Industrial Relations*, Vol VIII, p. 393, 1970.

Blanchflower David G. and Andrew J. Oswald. "Internal and External Influences Upon Pay settlements". *British Journal of Industrial Relations*. vol 26, no 3, November 1988.

Blau, Peter, M. *Exchange and Power in Social Life*. New York: John Wiley & Sons, Inc, 1964.

Broström Anders ed. *Storkonflikten 1980*. Stockholm: Arbetslivscentrum, 1981.

Brown E.H. Phelps *The Economics of Labor* New Haven 1962.

Brown W. et al. "Product and Labour Markets in Wage Determination: Some Australian Evidence!". *British Journal of Industrial Relations*. vol 22, no 2, July 1984.

Brown W. *Piecework Bargaining*. London: 1973.

Bulmer, Martin ed. *Working Class Images of Society*. London: Routledge Kegan & Paul, 1975.

Burns, Tom R; Svein Andersen, Thormud Lunde, Atle Midtun. *Organizational Change and Inertia*. Unpublished manuscript. Uppsala: Uppsala University Department of Sociology, 1984.

Burns, Tom R; Tom Baumgartner; Philippe DeVille. *Man, Decisions, and Society*, London: Gordon and Breach, 1985.

Burns, Tom R. and Anders S.Olsson. *The Swedish Model in Transition: Complexity Tension and Social Change in a Neo-corporatist System*. Uppsala: Department of Sociology Report, 1986.

Burns, Tom R. and Helena Flam. *The Shaping of Social Organization*. London: SAGE, 1987.

Casparsson, Ragnar. *LO Under fem årtionden*. Part 1. Stockholm: Tiden, 1947.

Casparsson, Ragnar. *LO Under fem årtionden*. Part 2. Stockholm: Tiden, 1948.

Chamberlain, Neil, W. *Collective Bargaining*. New York: McGraw- Hill Book Company, Inc, 1951.

Clegg H. *Trade Unionism Under Collective Bargaining: A Theory Based on Comparision of Six Countries*. Oxford: 1976.

Croner Fritz. *Tjänstemannakåren i det moderna samhället*. Uppsala: 1951.

Dabscheck  B. "Of Mountains and Routes over them: a Survey of Theories in Industrial Relations". *Journal of Industrial Relations* 25, 1983, pp. 485-506.

Dahlström Kjell-Åke. *Löneglidning*. Stockholm: SAF 1969.

DeGeer, Hans. *SAF i förhandlingar*. Svenska arbetsgivarföreningen och dess förhandlingsrelationer till LO och tjänstemannaorganisationerna 1930-1970. Stockholm: SAF 1986.

DeVille, Philippe and Tom R. Burns. "Institutional Responses to Crisis in Capitalist Development", *Social Praxis*, No 4, 1977.

Dunlop, John T. Wage Determination under Trade Unions. New York: Augustus M. Kelley Publishers, 1966. (Original edition 1944)

Dunlop, John, T. *Industrial Relations Systems*. New York: Henry Holt and Company, 1958.

Edgren G., K-O Faxén and C-E Odhner. *Lönebildning och samhällsekonomi*. Stockholm: Rabén & Sjögren , 1970.

Elvander, Nils. *Intresseorganisationerna i dagens Sverige*. 2nd Edition. Lund: CWK Gleerup Bokförlag, 1969.

Elvander, Nils. *Den Svenska Modellen: Löneförhandlingar och inkomstpolitik 1982-1986*. Stockholm: Allmänna Förlaget, 1988.

Eskilsson Sture, *Löneutveckling under kontroll*, Stockholm: SAF, 1966.

Finlay William. "Industrial Relations and Firm Behavior: Informal Labor Practices in the West Coast Longshore Industry". *Administrative Science Quarterly*, vol 32, pp 49-67, 1987.

Flanders Allan, ed. *Collective Bargaining*. Harmondsworth: Penguin Books Ltd, 1969.

Fredholm Eva. *Sin lön värd*. Gothenburg: Monographs from the Department of Sociology University of Gothenburg, no 41, 1989.

Freeman R.B. and J. Medoff, *What Do Unions Do*. New York: Basic Books, 1984

Fulcher James. "On the Explanation of Industrial Relations Diversity: Labour Movements, Employers and the State in Britain and Sweden". *British Journal of Industrial Relations*. vol 26, no 2, July 1988.

Förlikningsmannaexpeditionen. *Strike statistics*, various years.

Galtung Johan. *Theory and Methods of Sociological Research*, Oslo: Universitetsförlaget, 1970.

Giddens A, *The Constitution of Society*, Oxford: Polity Press, 1984.

Goffman, Erving. *Frame Analysis*. Middlesex: Penguin Books, 1975.

Habermas, Jürgen, *Legitimation Crisis*. London: Heineman, 1976.

Hadenius, Axel. *Facklig organisationsutveckling*. Stockholm: Raben & Sjögren, 1976.

Hansen Bent and Rehn Gösta, "On Wage Drift", in *25 Economic Essays in Honour of Erik Lindahl*, Stockholm: Ekonomisk Tidskrift, 1956.

Hart Horst and Casten von Otter. *Lönebildningen på arbetsplatsen*, Stockholm: Prisma och SOFI, 1973.

Hedström Peter. "Organisationsstruktur och lönebildning: En ekonomisk-sociologisk analys". *Sociologisk forskning 1*,1986.

Hirschman Albert O. *Exit, Voice, and Loyalty*, Cambridge: Harvard University Press 1970.

Hodson Randy and Robert L. Kaufman. "Economic Dualism: A Critical Review." *American Sociological Review*, vol 47, pp 727-739, 1982.

Holmlund, Bertil. *Labor Mobility: Studies of Labor Turnover and Migration in the Swedish Labor Market*. Stockholm: IUI, 1984

Holmlund Bertil and Per Skedinger. *Wage Bargaining and Wage Drift: Evidence from the Swedish Wood Industry*. Working Paper 1988:8 Uppsala: Department of Economics, 1988.

Howard William A. and N. Arnold Tolles. "Wage Determination in Key Manufacturing Industries, 1950-70". *Industrial & Labor Relations Review*, Vol 27, no 4, July 1974.

Hyman R. A Review Symposium. *Industrial Relations* 21, 1982, pp. 110-114.

Hyman Richard and Ian Brough. *Social Values and Industrial Realtions. A Study of Fairness and Inequality*. Oxford 1975.

Jacobsson, L. and A. Lindbeck. "Labour Market Conditions, Wages and Inflation. Swedish Experiences 1955-67". *Swedish Journal of Economics*, 71, 1969, pp 64-103.

Jacobsson, L. and A. Lindbeck. "On the Transmission Mechanism of Wage Change". *Swedish Journal of Economics*, 73, 1971, pp 273-293.

Jaques Elliott. *Measurement of Responsibility: A Study of Work, Payment, and Individual Capacity*. London: Tavistock Publications Ltd, 1956.

Johannesson Conny. *De centrala avtalsförhandlingarna och den fackliga demokratin*. Lund: Studentlitteratur 1975.

Johnston T.L. *Collective Bargaining in Sweden*. London: George Allen and Unwin Ltd , 1962.

Kjellberg Anders, *Facklig organisering i tolv länder*. Lund: Arkiv 1983.

Korpi W. and M. Shalev "Strikes, Industrial Relations and Class Conflict" *British Journal of Sociology* 30, 1979.

Korpi, Walter. "Conflict and the Balance of Power". *Acta Sociologica*. Vol 17, no 2, 1974.

Korpi, Walter. *Arbetarklassen i Välfärdskapitalismen*. Kristianstad: Bokförlaget Prisma, 1978.

Korpi Walter and Rune Åberg. *Marknad eller politik? Om de politiska alternativen i 80-talets Sverige*. Stockholm: LO, 1985.

Korpi, Walter. *The Democratic Class Struggle*. London: Routledge & Kegan Paul, 1983.

KTK: *Personal och lönepolitiskt program*. Stockholm: KTK, 1979.

Lash Scott. "The End of Neo-corporatism?: The Breakdown of Centralized Bargaining in Sweden". *British Journal of Industrial Relations*, Vol 23, No 2, July 1985.

LO: *Fackföreningsrörelsen och den fulla sysselsättningen*. Stockholm: LO 1951.

LO: *Lönepolitik: Rapport till LO-kongressen 1971*. Stockholm: LO, 1971.

LO: *Lönepolitik för 80-talet: Rapport till LO-kongressen 1981*. Stockholm: LO, 1981.

LO: *LO-nytt* no 7, February 1981.

LO: *Bakgrund och Fakta, Avtalsrörelsen 1983*, Stockholm: LO, 1983.

LO: *Avtalsrörelsen 1984*. Stockholm: LO, 1984

LO: *Verksamhetsberättelse 1984*, Stockholm: LO, 1985.

LO: *Gemensamt Ansvar för Arbete: Rapport till 1986 års LO-kongress från LOs utredning om arbete*. Stockholm: LO, 1986.

LO: *Lönepolitisk delrapport*. Stockholm: LO, 1987.

Lockwood David, "Sources of Variation in Working Class Images of Society" in Bulmer, Martin ed. *Working-Class Images of Society*, London: Routledge Kegan & Paul, 1975.

Long James E. and Albert N. Link. "The Impact of Market Structure on Wages, Fringe Benefits, and Turnover" *Industrial & Labor Relations Review*, Vol 36, no 2, January 1983.

Lyttkens, Lorentz. *Människors möten*. Lund: Doxa, 1981.

Marsden R. Industrial Relations: A Critique of Empiricism. *Sociology* 16, 1982, 232-250

Martin Andrew. "Trade Unions in Sweden: Strategic Responses to Change and Crisis". in Gourevitch et al. *Unions and Economic Crisis: Britain, West Germany and Sweden*. London: George Allen & Unwin, 1984.

Meidner, Rudolf. "Samordning och solidarisk lönepolitik under tre decennier". in *Tvärsnitt* . Stockholm:LO and Prisma, 1973.

Micheletti, Michele. *Central Labor Market Organizations and Politics*. Stockholm: University of Stockholm, Department of Political Science, 1983.

Michels Robert. *Organisationer och demokrati*. Stockholm: Timbro, 1983.

Miller David. *Social Justice*. Oxford: Oxford University Press, 1976.

Mishel Lawrence. "The Structural Determinants of Union Bargaining Power". *Industrial & Labor Relations Review*, Vol 40, no 1 October 1986.

Nagel, Jack, H. *The Descriptive Analysis of Power*. New Haven and London: Yale University Press, 1975.

Nash, J. F., Jr. "The Bargaining Problem". *Econometrica*. Vol 18, pp. 155-162, 1950.

Navarro Peter. "Union Bargaining Power in the Coal Industry, 1945-1981". *Industrial & Labor Relations Review*, Vol 36, no 2, January 1983.

Nilsson Christian and Johnny Zetterberg. *Lönestruktur och strukturella arbetsmarknadsproblem: Bilaga 10 till Långtidsutredningen 1987* Stockholm: Department of Finance, 1987a.

Nilsson Christian. *Lokal lönebildning och löneinflation*. Stockholm: FIEF, 1987.

Nilsson Tommy. *Från kamratförening till facklig rörelse*. Lund: Arkiv, 1985.

Nordin Rune, *Fackföreningsrörelsen i Sverige I: Uppkomst och utveckling*. Stockholm: Prisma, 1981.

Nordin Rune, *Den Fackliga arbetarrörelsen II: Organisation - verksamhet- samhälle. Stockholm*: Tidens förlag, 1983.

Norgren P. H. *The Swedish Collective Bargaining System* Harvard: Harvard University Press,1941

Nycander, Svante. *Kurs på Kollision*. Helsingfors: Askild & Kärnekull, 1972.

Offe Claus. *Disorganized Capitalism*. Cambridge: Polity Press, 1985.

Olsson, Anders S. Madeleine Wänseth. *Det svenska löneförhandlingssystemet*. Uppsala: Uppsala University, Department of Sociology, 1984.

Olsson Anders S. *Case studies for the Wage Negotiation project*. Uppsala: Department of Sociology, 1986.

Olsson Anders S., *Local-Central Dynamics in Wage Negotiation Systems and the Theories of Mancur Olson*, Uppsala: Department of Sociology, 1989.

Oswald Andrew. "The Economic Theory of Trade Unions: An Introductory Survey", *The Scandinavian Journal of Economics*, Vol 87, no 2, 1985.

Peterson Richard B. "Swedish Collective Bargaining - A Changing Scene". *British Journal of Industrial Relations*, Vol 25, No 1, March 1987.

Poole M. "A Power Analysis of Workplace Labour Relations", *Industrial Relations Journal* Vol 7, No 3, 1976, pp 31-43.

Provis Chris, "Comparative Wage Justice". *The Journal of Industrial relations*. Vol 28, No 1, March 1988.

Raiffa Howard. *The Art and Science of Negotiation*. Cambridge: Harvard University Press, 1982

Reynolds Lloyd G. *The Structure of Labor Markets*. New York: Harper & Brothers, 1951.

Reynaud J.D. "Conflict and Social Regulation", *British Journal of Industrial Relations*, Vol XVII, No 3, Nov 1979.

Roche William K. "Systems Analysis and Industrial Relations", *Economic and Industrial Democracy*, Vol 7, pp. 3-28, 1986.

Roomkin M. "Union Structure, Internal Control, and Strike Activity" *Industrial and Labor Relations* Review Vol 29, 1975/1976 pp. 198-217.

Rose M. "Universalism, Culturalism and the Aix Group: Promise and Problems of as Societal Approach to Economic Institutions" *European Sociological Review* 1(1):65-83.

Ross Arthur M. *Trade Union Wage Policy*. Berkeley: University of California Press, 1948.

Rundblad Bengt G. *Arbetskraftens rörlighet*. Stockholm: IUI, 1964.

Sabel George F. "The Internal Politics of Trade Unions". in Berger Suzanne ed. *Organizing Interests in Western Europe*, Cambridge: Cambridge University Press, 1981.

SACO/SR: *Inkomstpolitiskt program*, SACO/SR:s programskrifter -79 års kongress nr 3. Stockholm, SACO/SR, 1980.

SAF/LOs gemensamma statistiknämnd: *Löneglidningen inom SAF/LO-området*. Stockholm: SAF, 1982.

SAF: Annual Reports 1962-1982.

SAF: *Rättvis lön - lönepolitiskt program*. Stockholm: SAF, 1979.

SAF: *Löneutveckling för arbetare och tjänstemän vid några företag*. Stockholm: SAF 1980.

SAF: Promemoria 1980-09-03.

SAF: Letter dated 1981-03-06.

SAF: *Lönespridning arbetare tjänstemän 1972-1980*. Stockholm: SAF, 1981

SAF: Promemoria 1982-05-04.

SAF: Statutes 1982-06-29.

SAF: *Indexreglering av löner samt följsamhetsregler mellan olika löntagarkollektiv i Sverige: SAFs bidrag till nordisk utredning*. Stockholm: SAF, 1982.

SAF: *Tjänstemännens lönestatistik* Augusti 1982. Stockholm: SAF, 1982b.

SAF: *Fakta om Sveriges ekonomi 1983*. Stockholm: SAF, 1983.

SAF: *Arbetsgivaravgifter enligt lagar och avtal 1960-1984*. Stockholm: SAF 1984.

SAF: *Fakta om Sveriges ekonomi 1986*. Stockholm: SAF, 1986.

Sandberg Per. *Tjänstemannarörelsen*. Stockholm: 1969.

SCB: *Perspektiv på välfärden: Levnadsförhållanden Nr 33, översikt SOS*. Stockholm: Liber/allmänna förlaget, 1982.

SCB: *Statistical Abstracts of Sweden 1954*. Stockholm: SCB, 1954.

SCB: *Statistical Abstracts of Sweden 1955*. Stockholm: SCB, 1955.

SCB: *Statistical Abstracts of Sweden 1956*. Stockholm: SCB, 1956.

SCB: *Statistical Abstracts of Sweden 1957*. Stockholm: SCB, 1957.

SCB: *Statistical Abstracts of Sweden 1958*. Stockholm: SCB, 1958.

SCB: *Statistical Abstracts of Sweden 1962*. Stockholm: SCB, 1962.

SCB: *Statistical Abstracts of Sweden 1963*. Stockholm: SCB, 1963.

SCB: *Statistical Abstracts of Sweden 1984*. Stockholm: SCB, 1984.

SCB: *Statistical Reports 1969: P1969:21*. Stockholm: SCB, 1969.

SCB: *Yearbook of Labor Statistics* 1974. Stockholm: SCB, 1975.

SCB: *Yearbook of Labor Statistics* 1982-83. Stockholm: Liber, 1983.

Schager Nils Henric. "Den lokala lönebildningen och företagens vinster - en preliminär analys" in *SOU 1979:10*. Stockholm: Liber, 1979.

Schager Nils Henric. "The Duration of Vacancies as a Measure of the State of Demand in the Labour Market. The Swedish Wage Drift Equation Reconsidered", in Eliasson et al. (eds.) *Studies of Labour Market Behavior: Sweden and the United States*. Conference Report 1981:2. Stockholm: IUI, 1981.

Schager Nils Henric. "Den lokala lönebildningen och företagens vinster - en preliminär analys". *SOU 1982:47*. Stockholm: Liber, 1982.

Schager Nils Henric. *Unemployment, Vacancy Durations and Wage Increases: Application of Markov Processes to Labour Market Dynamics*. Research Report no 29 1987. Stockholm: IUI, 1987.

Schager Nils Henric. *Causes of Wage Drift in Swedish Manufacturing: a Remarkable Case of Regular Behaviour.* IUI. Stockholm: IUI, 1988.

Scheinstock G. "Towards a Theory of Industrial Relations". *British Journal of Industrial Relations.* Volume 19, No 2, July 1981.

Schelling, Thomas, C. *The Strategy of Conflict.* New York: Oxford University Press, 1970.

Scott Richard W. *Organizations: Rational, Natural, and Open Systems.* Enlewood Cliffs, Prentice-Hall Inc., 1981.

SIF: *SIFs lönepolitik.* Stockholm: TCO, 1976

SIF: General Council minutes, 1983-05-17.

SIF: General Council minutes, 1983-09-07.

SIND: *Vinster och sysselsättning i Svensk industri: En strukturanalys av Sveriges Industri 1969-1977. Utredning 1980:2*, Stockhom: Liber, 1980.

Solow Robert M. "Insiders and Outsiders in Wage Determination". *Scandinavian Journal of Economics*, Vol 87, no 2, 1985.

Stevens, Carl, M. *Strategy and Collective Bargaining Negotiation.* Westport, Conn.: Greenwood Press, Publishers, 1963.

Strauss George and Peter Feuille, "Industrial Relations Research: A Critical Analysis" *Industrial Relations* 17 (3), 1978, pp. 259-77.

Strauss, Anselm. *Negotiations.* San Francisco: Josey-Bass Publishers, 1978.

Ståhl, Ingolf. *Bargaining Theory.* Stockholm: EFI,1972.

Suarez Pablo and Goldborne Gladys, "The Electoral Consequences of the Enfranchisement of Women: Problems, Hypotheses and Methodological Approaches". Paper presented at the 28th World Congress of the International Institute of Sociology, Albufeira, Portugal, 1986.

Sunesson, Sune. *Politik och organisation.* Lund: Arkiv, 1974.

Swedberg Richard, Ulf Himmelstrand and Göran Brulin. "The Paradigm of Economic Sociology: Premises and Promises." *Research Reports from the Department of Sociology Uppsala University*, Vol 1985:1

TCO: *Lönepolitiken inom tjänstemannarörelsen*, Stockholm: TCO, 1963.

TCO: *Tjänstemännens lönepolitik.* Stockholm: TCO, 1973.

TCO: *Lönepolitikens samhällsekonomiska förutsättningar.* Stockholm: TCO, 1982.

TCO: *Förslag till program för TCO 1985-1988.* Stockholm: TCO, 1985.

TCO: *Gemensam löneutveckling: en debattskrift om löneglidning*. Stockholm: TCO, 1987.

Thibaut, John, W.; Harold H. Kelley. *The Social Psychology of Groups*. New York: John Wiley & Sons, 1959.

Turnbull Peter J. "The Economic Theory of Trade Union Behaviour: A Critique". *British Journal of Industrial Relations*, Vol 26, no 1, March 1988.

Turner Steve, *Strong Trade Unions, Corporatism and Economic Performance: A Critical Review of the Literature*. Stockholm: IUI and Harvard University, 1985.

Ullenhag, Jörgen. *Den solidariska lönepolitiken i Sverige*. Stockholm: Läromedelsförlagen, 1971.

Victorin, Anders. *Lönenormering genom kollektivavtal*. Stockholm: Allmänna Förlaget, 1973.

Walton, Richard, E. ; Robert B. McKersie. *A Behavioural Theory of Labor Negotiations*. New York: McGraw-Hill Book Company, 1965.

Westerståhl, Jörgen. *Svensk fackföreningsrörelse*. Stockholm: Tidens förlag, 1945.

Wood S. "Ideology in Industrial Relations Theory" *Industrial Relations Journal* Vol 9 No 4 42-56.

Zeuthen, F. *Problems of Monopoly and Economic Warfare*. London: Routledge & Kegan Paul, 1930.

Åberg Rune and Walter Korpi. *Marknad eller politik: Om de politiska alternativen i 80-talets Sverige*. Stockholm: LO 1985.

Åmark Klas. *Facklig makt och fackligt medlemskap*. Lund: Arkiv, 1986.